GOOD
VINTAGE

GOOD VINTAGE

A Wine Lover's Companion

Simon Cadell

Special Edition for PAST TIMES®, Oxford England

First published as *The Right Vintage* in Great Britain in 1995 by Robson Books Ltd., Bolsover House, 5-6 Clipstone Street, London W1P 8LE.

British Library Cataloguing in Publication data
A catalogue record for this title is available from the British Library.

ISBN 1 86105 069 0

Book designed by Harold King

Book set in Bembo by Pitfold Design, Hindhead.
Printed in Great Britain by St Edmundsbury Press, Bury St Edmunds, Suffolk.

This book is dedicated to my wife Beckie,
my two sons Patrick and Alec,
and my wine merchant Trevor Hughes

INTRODUCTION

I bought my first bottle of wine for rather different reasons than I buy wine today. I tend to romanticize this story by saying I was about fourteen at the time, but I know I must have been older than that. I've always looked older than I am, a characteristic which is useful and fun in extreme youth, less alluring in middle age; I was offered an OAP ticket the other day at a station I use three or four times a week. Maybe I'd had too much wine the night before.

My parents lived in Hampstead, North London, and there opened in the early sixties in the village something of a novelty for those days, a specialist independent wine merchant. It was called the Hampstead Wine Company. I walked past it quite often since it was almost next door to the Everyman Cinema, where my uncle used to take me to see Marx Brothers movies. The cinema screen had no curtain. Instead the screen itself was lit in a distinctive shade of green. There we sat in green dimness waiting for the film to start and my uncle would start to laugh in anticipation of what he was about to see. It was (and is) an infectious laugh and quite often I and the rest of the small audience would be chortling away as the film began. It was at this cinema that I saw many classic films for the first time, including a late-night showing of *Casablanca*. A packed audience of aficionados greeted the entrance of major characters with a short but intensive round of applause and at the end there was a thunderous ovation lasting several minutes as though the audience were trying to reach through the screen and beyond the intervening years to thank those responsible for their enjoyment.

But I digress – back to the subject in hand.

From the outside the Hampstead Wine Company looked very chic. Inside there was a wooden floor and the walls were lined with wooden wine bins, each one containing a dozen or more bottles of a particular wine. One day I ventured in and browsed amongst the bins, but I had no idea what I was looking for. Then I saw a strange three-sided bottle with a rather handsome label, so for no better reason than its look I bought it, and what a happy choice it was. The wine was Château Rauson-Segla. My parents and I drank it the following Sunday. I had never tasted anything like it, a depth, roundness and subtlety that is still etched on my palate's memory.

It was a long time before I drank wine of such quality again. As a student at drama school I couldn't afford it and neither could I most of my time as a young actor. When I occasionally got a 'tele', then as now much better paid than the theatre, I would seek out a good wine merchant and buy a bottle of this and a bottle of that, take it home, taste it, drink it and try to learn from it. By the end of the seventies I had acquired a considerable knowledge of what I liked and disliked. (I adore Chardonnay, my desert island luxury would have to be white Burgundy, and I dislike the Gamay grape so Beaujolais is a closed book to me.) Knowledge I was acquiring – yes; but wine – no. I was not yet earning enough to buy more than I drank. Even if I had been, I had nowhere to store it.

Then in the late seventies and early eighties my fortunes improved. The flat I lived in in Notting Hill Gate was redecorated and as part of this process I had built into the kitchen a boxed wine-storage area, vented into the outside wall and holding about 350 bottles and 100 magnums. Yet sadly they remained pretty much empty for quite some time, for there was a piece of the jigsaw missing: I didn't know a good wine merchant.

My then boss and now happily my father-in-law is David Croft. He and his wife Anne have a large and very beautiful medieval farmhouse in Suffolk. On my very first visit there for a Saturday lunch David said, 'I'll just get some wine from the cellar.' Intrigued, I went with him.

Under the first rise of the main staircase in the house there is a door secured by a massive old lock. The key is turned, a light switched on and you go down surprisingly broad stone stairs which turn sharply to the left at the bottom. You are then confronted by a most handsome cellar, stone-flagged, semi-vaulted and semi-beamed. There has been a house on the site since the beginning of the thirteenth century and I'm sure the cellar, whatever its original use, has always been there. And the smell! It's the same in old cellars the world over – a slightly sweet and sour mustiness. It's unique and I love it.

David selected some wine and on the way back up the stairs I asked, 'Who's your wine merchant?'

'Nobody in particular,' he said. 'The Wine Society, and other than that I buy where and when the fancy takes me.'

Beckie, then my girlfriend, now (fortunate man that I am) my wife, and I were regular weekend visitors to Suffolk, and I always made sure that I brought up from London four or six bottles of good wine. One weekend Beckie travelled up separately. I had driven beyond Bury St Edmunds when I realized that, without her to remind me, I'd forgotten the wine. Should I turn back to Bury, or be adventurous and go on past the house to Thetford which was then uncharted territory to me. I settled for Thetford.

My heart sank as I arrived. Thetford is one of the those many ancient market towns whose very heart was vandalized in the late fifties and early sixties by the town planners. I parked my car in the inevitable precinct car park. At the exit from the precinct was a branch of a well-known chain of wine merchants. Oh well, I thought, and walked sullenly towards the door.

Some unknown instinct saved me. I glanced down the street to my left and about sixty or seventy yards away on the other side of the road was a black sign with gold lettering proclaiming T & W Wines. Drawn down the street, I entered an Aladdin's cave for wine lovers. Trevor Hughes who owns and runs the company said that my communication on that first meeting was limited almost entirely to 'Oh my God!', 'I don't believe it!' as one treasure after another beckoned to me from the bins. I'd found my wine merchant.

Trevor Hughes is about six feet tall, not fat, but to use a cricketing term 'well-covered'. He has a contagious laugh which I can only describe as being like a very happy man falling backwards off a tall building. It starts in an explosive crescendo and quickly fades to nothing. He is entirely self-taught and his knowledge is astounding. My friend, director Peter Farago, is Hungarian by birth and thought he would try to catch Trevor out. He had rung his father, a gentleman of such old Middle European charm that it is a pleasure simply to be in the same room as him, and asked him for the name of a little-known Hungarian wine. After about half an hour of tasting and talking, Peter said casually, 'Do you know a wine called . . . ?' (I can't remember the name.) Without pause Trevor replied, 'Hungarian of course, and rather good, particularly if you like eucalyptus'.

Peter and I were astounded.

'You see,' Trevor continued, 'two sides of the vineyard are surrounded by eucalyptus trees. The prevailing wind comes from these sides and you can taste it in the wine.'

There's a saying about Hungarians that they are the only people who can enter a revolving door behind you and come out in front. This is the only time I have seen the situation reversed.

I owe Trevor an enormous debt of gratitude, for it is under his guidance and tutelage over the last fourteen years that I have increased my knowledge and enjoyment of wine and while doing so built up a rather good cellar.

Let me pass on a few quick tips about buying and drinking wine. First supermarket wines.

Nowadays most large supermarket chains have wonderful wine buyers working for them; there's no problem there. Where there is a snag is with the wine in the shops where it is stored upright, usually under the glare of fluorescent lighting (a great enemy of wine) and at a temperature of about 75°F or 24°C. After four or five weeks in these conditions any wine will start to deteriorate, and how can you know whether the wine you want to buy has been standing on the shelves for that long, or even longer? The solution is easily within the supermarkets' grasp, I only hope that soon they do something about it.

The only practical advice I can offer is that whenever you buy wine never ever buy a bottle where the cork has started to push up the lead. Run your thumb across the top of the bottle. It should feel absolutely flat, even slightly concave.

If buying from a wine merchant you don't know, select your wine from the shelf then ask the merchant if you could have a similar bottle from his storeroom. If the proffered bottle is at all warm to the touch, go elsewhere.

This may sound a bit pedantic but I cannot stress enough that wine is a living thing as much in the bottle as on the vine. Treat it badly and a great wine becomes mediocre and a good wine undrinkable.

It's useful also to learn something about the notation given on the wine label. This is quite easy and, particularly with European wines, tells you an awful lot.

Drinking wines in restaurants, a golden rule: the wine you've ordered should be brought to the table unopened and opened in front of you. If it is to be decanted the same rule applies; it must be decanted at the table. The most surprising places are not above chicanery. I was lunching at a rather grand London club a month or two ago. My hostess asked me to order the wine, which I did, asking for a good Puligny-Montrachet. Some minutes later the wine arrived at the table – opened. If I hadn't been a guest I would have sent it straight back, as it was I tasted it; it was not Puligny-Montrachet. I said to the waiter that the wine wasn't good and could the next bottle be brought to the table unopened and opened in front of us. The waiter disappeared and soon returned with the unopened bottle, but now said, 'I can't open it here – the corkscrew is fixed in the bar next door'. Not the only thing that's fixed in the bar, I thought.

'Fine,' I said, 'but hang on a minute.' I got out a pen and signed my name across the label – simple, but effective.

If you get to know a restaurant that is obviously as interested in its wines as its food, as all restaurants should be, then ask the person who takes the wine order for advice. This can produce many delightful surprises. In grander establishments you will be confronted by the rather daunting figure of the sommelier, black-tied, cut-away frock coat with brass buttons and a silver chain on which hangs a silver wine taster, waistcoat and a crisp white apron covering the waist to just above the knee. A quick test in assessing the sommelier's attitude is to ask him what he thinks you should drink with the meat course. If he immediately points to the most expensive red wine in the list, ignore him. If on the other hand he asks what meat you are going to have, then flicks thoughtfully through the list and comes up with a wine that you may or may not know, trust him.

Some years ago I went for the first time to Roger Vergé's Moulin de Mougins. The great man himself was cooking and it remains the best meal I've had outside England. (Outside England? Yes, Raymond Blanc's Manoir aux Quat' Saisons is a very hard act to follow.) The sommelier at the Moulin de Mougins was charming but it wasn't till the pudding was about to arrive that I asked his advice. 'What dessert wines do you have?'

'We have no Sauternes or Barsac,' he replied, 'but we do have a sweet wine from the Loire.'

I happened to know it and said, 'We'll have a bottle of that, please.' The feast ended triumphantly.

The food and wine had been so good that about ten days later we went again. Now the Moulin de Mougins is not a small restaurant. There must be a hundred covers and in the summer months it is packed both for lunch and dinner. There are several multi-choice menus and this time we chose from a different one to our previous visit. The sommelier arrived and said, 'I understand you are eating from a different menu tonight. May I suggest one change from the wines you drank last time?'

'Of course,' I said, and was introduced to Château de Beaucastel Châteauneuf-du-Pape. I never had to mention the other wines: they arrived course after course, including at the end the sweet wine from the Loire. Such dedication, enthusiasm and customer care are not as uncommon as you might think in the world of wine.

Now for temperature. Don't serve white wines too cold, it's impossible to taste them if you do. If in a restaurant the white wine comes in an ice bucket and at first taste is icy then ask for it to be taken out and left on the table. It will soon warm up a bit and you will enjoy it much more. Ice buckets are really only useful if drinking outside on a hot summer's day. Sweet whites should be drunk a little cooler than dry whites.

Don't serve red wines too warm. If you discover as you pour the red that it is a bit cold, then pour a generous amount into each glass and in about ten minutes it will be fine. Never try to increase the temperature of red wine quickly – no putting in front of the fire, into sinks of hot water, next to radiators or on the top of the stove. It will taste as if it has been microwaved.

Decanting: I'm not a great believer in this and it should certainly never be done with really old wines. These must be opened and drunk immediately, otherwise the wine's first taste of air for forty or more years quickly fades it. Some wines improve with decanting; a lot improve by opening twenty minutes to an hour before drinking. If you're going to do this, open the bottle and pour a good third of a glass. This you can taste, of course, and it allows more air into the bottle, which is the object of the exercise in the first place.

Finally, a little about the book itself. It's a collection of writings about wine over the centuries: some only a few lines, some short essays. Some are funny, some informative, some sentimental but never sad.

The publishers asked me to nominate with each extract a wine I thought might be a suitable accompaniment. The wines I have chosen are largely ones I have tasted and enjoyed. There are many entries in the book – don't drink too quickly!

Cheers.

If on my theme I rightly think,
There are five reasons why men drink,
Good wine, a friend, or being dry,
Or lest we should be, by and by,
Or any other reason why.

From the Latin of Henry Aldrich, Dean of Christ Church College,
Oxford (1689-1710)

This charming verse contains a vital message: you don't need an excuse to drink a glass of wine! I think a good slurping wine should be drunk with this, so I recommend a New Zealand Sauvignon Blanc. Try one called Jackson Estate.

Often wine has shown me matters in their true perspective, and has, as though by the touch of a magic wand, reduced great disasters to small inconveniences.

Wine has lit up for me the pages of literature, and revealed in life romance lurking in the commonplace.

Wine has made me bold but not foolish; has induced me to say silly things but not to do them.

Duff Cooper *Old Men Forget*, 1953

What superbly concise use of the language – not a word wasted. A glass of champagne with Duff Cooper . . . my own favourite is Michel Arnould et fils Grand Cru from Verzenay.

Drinking

The thirsty Earth soaks up the Rain,
And drinks, and gapes for drink again.
The Plants suck in the Earth, and are
With constant drinking fresh and fair.
The Sea it self, which one would think
Should have but little need of Drink,
Drinks ten thousand Rivers up,
So fill'd that they o'rflow the Cup.
The busie Sun (and one would guess
By's drunken fiery face no less)
Drinks up the Sea, and when h'as done,
The Moon and Stars drink up the Sun.
They drink and dance by their own light,
They drink and revel all the night.
Nothing in Nature's Sober found,
But an eternal Health goes round.
Fill up the Bowl then, fill it high,
Fill all the Glasses there, for why
Should every Creature drink but I,
Why, Men of Morals, tell me why?

Abraham Cowley (1618-67)

This elegant and logical verse raises the guilt question. People who don't drink have the idea that drinkers drink to get drunk and because all drinkers have, on occasion, had one over the eight and suffered for it, a sediment of guilt enters the drinker's consciousness. This guilt must be treated as nothing more than it is – part of a hangover.

There is also, to mitigate any remaining doubt, the smugly satisfying recent research which shows that moderate wine drinking is very good for you. So a robust Bordeaux: Château Moulinet from Pomerol.

Wine gives you joy; love, grief and tortures, besides surgeons. Wine makes us witty: love only sots. Wine makes us sleep; love breaks it.

William Wycherley *The Country Wife*, 1675

I'm not sure I entirely agree, but a bottle of Aloxe-Corton 'Les Mourottes' from Beaune will oil any discussion very nicely.

from Ode to a Nightingale

O for a draught of vintage! that hath been
Cooled a long age in the deep-delved earth,
Tasting of Flora and the country-green,
Dance, and Provençal song, and sunburnt mirth!
O for a beaker full of the warm South!
Full of the true, the blushful Hippocrene,
With beaded bubbles winking at the brim,
And purple-stained mouth;
That I might drink, and leave the world unseen,
And with thee fade into the forest dim . . .

John Keats, 1818

'O for a beaker full of the warm South!' – what a wonderful line. Without leaving France you can't get much further south than Provence so try a Bandol AOC: I recommend Moulin des Costes. Bandol wines are underrated at the moment – they may not be for long!

Recipe for wine sop

Here are declared .iiij. commodites of wyne soppis. The fyrst is / they purge the tethe / by reason they stycke longer in the tethe / than wyne alone or bread alone: therfore the fylthynes of the tethe is the better consumed / and the tethe the better purged. The .ij. comodite is / that it sharpeth the syghte: for it letteh the yll fumes to ascende to the brayne: which by th[e]yr mynglynge together / darke the syghte. And this is by reason that hit digesteth all ill matters beynge in the stomake. Thyrdly / hit digeste the perfectly meates nat well digested: for it closeth the mouthe of the stomake / and conforteth digestion. Fourthly / hit reducethe superfluous digestion to meane. All this is of trouthe / so that the breade sopped in wyne / be fyrste tosted or dryed on imbers.

Regimen Sanitatis Salerni, a medieval guide to healthy living

Wine as toothpaste, now there's a thought. It conjures up Colgate's Lafite and Maclean's Montrachet, and concerned assistants in chemist's shops saying, 'I don't think that one's quite ready for brushing yet, sir.'

I'm drawn to Rioja for my suggestion here. I'm not quite sure why, except that you can still get hold of very old vintages, not as old as the extract, but wines between thirty and forty years old are still available. Try an old red Marqués de Murrieta.

Were I to prescribe a rule for drinking, it should be formed upon a saying quoted by Sir William Temple: the first glass for myself, the second for my friends, the third for good humour, and the fourth for mine enemies.

Joseph Addison (1672-1719) from the Spectator, No. 195

Three glasses of Château Fuissé.

The art of taking wine is the science of exciting agreeable conversation and eliciting brilliant thoughts for an idle hour between the dining and the drawing room. Wine makes some men dull; such persons should on no account drink the strong brandied wines of the south, but confine themselves to the light red French growths, or to the white, pregnant with carbonic gas. If these fail to promote cheerfulness; if with the light Burgundy, with Lafite, or the ethereal sparkle of Champagne, a man continue unmoved, he may depend the innocent use of wine cannot be his. He may excite himself by the stronger kinds, and half intoxicate himself to raise a leaven of agreeability which is altogether artificial; – he may woo mirth 'sorrowfully' but he will only injure his stomach and cloud his brain. Oftentimes do Englishmen drink themselves into taciturnity below-stairs, and, ascending to the drawing-room, sit silent and solemn as so many quakers, among the fair sex. Such are past the stage of innocent excitement by a rational quantity of the juice of the grape. They take it because the effect is a temporary indifference, an agreeable suspense from pleasure and from pain. Such are not the true enjoyers of wine in its legitimate use; and they should always rise and retire with the ladies, for the effect upon them is that of a narcotic.

The true enjoyer of wine finds it exhilarate the spirits, increase the memory, promote cheerfulness; if he be something of a wit, it draws out his hoarded stores of good sayings and lively repartees, during the moment of relaxation from thought, at the hour when it is good 'to sit awhile'. This cheerful glass calls into action his better natural qualities, as with the ruby liquid he swallows 'a sunbeam of the sky'. He makes his wine secondary to his conversation, and when he finds the latter at what he thinks its keenest edge and brightest polish, he leaves the table to mingle with beauty, and exchange the wine for a sparkle of more attractive and higher character, perhaps to bask in 'the purple light of love'. He who would destroy good wine, by taking it when its flavour is no longer fresh to the palate, is a drunkard; he knows nothing of the refinement in animal enjoyment, which consists in taking rather less than enough. Always to rise from the feast with an appetite is a maxim which, however gourmands and sensualists may despise it, is a course for a rational being, as well as that which yields the richest enjoyment. By this we preserve the freshness of the first taste, the full flavour of the first sip: as the odour of the rose deadens upon the sense after the first exhalation, so is it with wine and all our enjoyments. Thus we learn how we may, in the truest and most refined sense, enjoy the pleasures by which the benevolence of Him who has given us the things enjoyed, is best repaid by our enjoying wisely.

Many who are of the earth, earthy, imagine as long as they get wine into the stomach it is no matter how the thing is done. Such persons may be styled 'stomach-drinkers', and may as well attain the lodgment of the fluid in the part desired by means of a forcing pump and a tube as any other mode. The palate to them is secondary to the warmth of this general magazine of liquids and solids. One of true vinographical taste must feel a horror at association over wine with such persons. A refinement even in our sins is better than the grossness of the coarser natures of mankind in animal vices. How much does this tell in innocent enjoyment. As Chesterfield felt when his son licked the plate at table, despite all his instructions in good breeding, it may be imagined how the man of refinement feels in the company of coarse, vulgar companions over wine. One half our pleasures are relative or conventional, and therefore this alloy in any mode turns them to pain.

The chief thing in the art of drinking wine, is to keep within those salutary limits which mark the beneficial from the pernicious. In good society, in the present day, this line is well defined; but a man must mingle in this distempered life with every class, and the difficulty is to keep the mean in those cases, where others have no regard to it. This is best done by studying self-respect, and the art of saying 'No', when the necessity for saying 'No' is strongly felt. The courage to do this, and that absence of all fear of being accounted singular – which it is a man's duty to cultivate, if he wish to be thought worthy of his species, will prevent his suffering in stomach or moral character from that table complaisance which the too pliant force upon themselves contrary to better feelings.

Cyrus Redding on the 'art of taking wine', 1833
Quoted in Charles Tovey *Wit, Wisdom and Morals:*
Distilled from Bacchus, 1878

The message is clear and I agree with it wholeheartedly: wine should be tasted and not just drunk. There are few things more irritating than giving a dinner party at which good wines are served and seeing one or two of your guests drinking them like water. My father-in-law has an answer to this situation. Having identified the 'drinkers' at a dinner party, he will go round with two bottles at a time, one a perfectly drinkable vin ordinaire and one fine bottle for those that appreciate it. The 'slurpers' to my knowledge have never realized what is being done – of course they don't, they are merely interested in swallowing. The other spin-off from this practice is that there is more good wine for those that love it!

Saying 'No', I find nowadays, is easier and easier. There was a time when if I was offered a glass of wine I'd take it. But now I find that bad wine makes me feel ill, not the next day, but while I'm drinking it. So if at some large party or function the wine is poor, I move quickly on to water or orange juice.

A wine that has an infinitely subtle panoply of tastes is Château de Beaucastel Châteauneuf-du-Pape. You can buy either red or white and it is quite delicious.

Wine is never monotonous, and he or she who will only take the trouble to look for it should be able to find just the right wine for the right company and occasion. There are wines of many hues from the palest amber to the deepest purple; there are still and sparkling wines, and yet others which are just lively, not quite still and not really sparkling; there are dry and sweet wines, a whole range of fine shades and degrees of sweetness; there are wines which contain so little alcohol that any teetotaller could drink them with a clear conscience, and there are also wines which are so potent that they must not be quaffed but sipped; there are wines which are quite delightful to drink freely within a year or two of their vintage, whilst others may live up to twenty-five, fifty, and even to a hundred years and still be a real joy for wine connoisseurs.

There is but one rule which needs to be remembered as regards the choice of different wines for different meals and occasions: 'The best wine is that which is the most suitable, hence the most pleasing at the time.' There are many rules concerning the service of wine, but none of them are binding, although most of them are reasonable. It is reasonable, for instance, to serve a bottle of a sweet white wine with a sweet dish, at the end of a meal, rather than with a roast grouse or a pork chop. It is reasonable to choose lighter wines to begin with and stronger, heavier wines to follow rather than to precede them, but the most reasonable thing of all is to find out what your guests would like and, if you have no guests, to make up your own mind what you think would be the most suitable, hence the best, wine.

Last, but by no means least, wine is best because it is the safest, pleasantest and most wholesome of all beverages. It is safer than water or milk: you cannot get typhoid or TB from any wine, be it old or young, cheap and nasty, or rare and costly. No microbes live in wine. It is pleasanter than other safe drinks because it is more gentle as well as more varied. There is no wine without any alcohol, since grape juice does not begin to be wine until it has fermented, and by then the sugar of the grape juice has become the alcohol of the wine. But the alcohol in wine is as the canvas upon which an artist paints a picture: it is there, of course, but you do not see it and do not think of it; it is not the canvas that you are interested in, but the picture which is on it. It is the same with wine; it is not the small percentage of alcohol that appeals to you, but the brilliant ruby of the wine's colour, the attractive perfume of its 'bouquet' and the delicious savour of its 'farewell', the lingering taste which it leaves behind as it descends smoothly down your grateful throat: that is the picture that is painted on the canvas of the wine's alcohol. Of course the alcohol is there all the time, and very welcome it is: it holds everything so well together: it diffuses such a comforting light and warmth; it provides the limelight which enables us to enjoy fully all the fine points of the wine's colour, bouquet and flavour. And it does it in a gentle fashion; it is never brutal; it never is treacherous, stabbing one in the back or in the brain as immature spirits do. Wine is 'a good familiar creature', as Shakespeare calls it, and Shakespeare always is right. Wine is a gentle stimulant, a good counsellor, a true friend, who neither bores nor irritates us: it does not send us to sleep, nor does it keep us awake; it never becomes a craving or a tyrant; it is always ready to cheer, to help, but not to bully us.

Wine is a friend, wine is a joy; and, like sunshine, wine is the birthright of all. It grows so freely and is so cheap that there is wine for all, rich and poor alike, in wine-producing lands and in all others. Wine is cheaper, where it is made, than oranges and lemons which, in England, are not the privilege of the rich. Wine is. Why? Simply because oranges and lemons come in free of duty whilst wine is taxed so heavily that none but the rich may enjoy its message of good health and good will. May the day come, and the sooner it comes the better for all, when wine will no longer be penalized as it is at present on reaching these shores, and when it will be once again within the reach of all.

André Simon *A Wine Primer*, 1946

Well, this really says it all and the analogy of canvas and painting to alcohol and wine is a stroke of genius.

A great wine with a great man – Château Margaux.

But at quite an early stage I learned one important lesson, and that is that the pleasure of wine consists only partly in itself; the good talk that is inseparable from a wine dinner is even more important than the wines that are being served. Never bring up your better bottles if you are entertaining a man who cannot talk. Keep your treasures for a night when those few who are nearest to your heart can gather round your table, free from care, with latchkeys in their pockets and no last train to catch.

Maurice Healy, *Claret and the White Wines of Bordeaux*, 1934

What did Mr Healy do with people he hadn't met before? I suppose if you went to dinner with him and started the evening with champagne quickly followed by a bottle of Black Tower you'd get the message pretty quickly that your conversation wasn't up to scratch.

I once went to a dinner party where one of the guests arrived in a severe state of drunkenness. Before dinner he sat in the drawing-room toying with a Scotch and saying not a word. We moved into the dining room and very soon he appeared to have fallen asleep. The dinner party went on perfectly happily around him. The conversation turned (I can't remember how) to C B Cochran, a legendary inter-war impresario known to everyone as Cocky, and particularly to his untimely and horrid death − he was scalded to death in his bath. At the mention of this a jolt went through the drunken guest . He opened his eyes, said, 'Hence the origin of the recipe Cock au Bain,' and returned immediately to his former state.

Assuming we're in Mr Healy's good books, how about a glass of Meursault Premier Cru.

If you intend to drink much *after* dinner, never drink much *at* dinner, and particularly avoid mixing wines. If you begin with Sauterne, for example, stick to Sauterne, though, on the whole, red wines are best. Avoid malt liquor most cautiously; for nothing is so apt to get into the head unawares, or, what is almost as bad, to fill the stomach with wind. Champagne, on the latter account, is bad. Port, three glasses at dinner – claret, three bottles after: behold the fair proportion, and the most excellent wines.

Sir Morgan O'Doherty, Bart *Maxims*

At first this seems quite sound advice. I agree about the malt liquor but disagree about the champagne, but then we come to Sir Morgan O'Doherty's recommended consumption: port, then three bottles of claret!
I think I'll stick to Sauternes, a glass of Château Gilette.

I have another mild pastime and that is a collection of soil and vine clippings from the major Grand Cru of Burgundy.
Imagine the pleasure and interest that can be given to those guests who are genuinely interested in being able to not only taste a great wine but to be able to compare the soil in which the vine has grown with its neighbours, etc. I wonder if any reader could coin a name for such a pastime.

R Rowan *Decanter* (quoted in *Private Eye*, 'Pseuds Corner')

Yes, it should be called Terminal Pretension. My drink recommendation is a glass of water.

At a restaurateur's, when you ask for any wine above the pitch of *vin ordinaire*, always examine the cork before you allow the *sommelier* to draw it. This is a maxim worth any money. The French have an odious custom of allowing people to have half bottles of the higher wines. The waiters, of course, fill up the bottle with an inferior sort, and seal it again; so that you frequently get your Sauterne christened with Chablis. I am sorry to he obliged to say, that at the *Rocher de Cancale*, this trick is very commonly played off. It certainly injures the respectability of the house, and even endangers the throne of the Bourbons. I ought here in gratitude to mention, that at *Prévot's,* one of the best of the second-rate restaurateurs, I have drunk delicious *Château grillé* – a wine very rarely found in the *cartes*.

Sir Morgan O'Doherty, Bart *Maxims*

Sound advice from Sir Morgan but the cheating of restaurant customers still goes on. It is outrageous when you think that the mark-up on wines in restaurants can be more than 300 per cent.

Château Grillet is a delicious white wine from the Northern Rhône. It's still hard to come by but well worth the hunt.

Water is not wholesome sole by itself for an Englishman. Good wine moderately drunken doth actuate and doth quicken a man's wits; it doth comfort his heart; it doth scour the liver; it doth engender good blood; it doth comfort and nourish the brain, wherefore it is medicinal.

I myself, which am a physician, cannot away with water, wherefore I do leave all water, and do take myself to good ale, and otherwhile for ale I do take good Gascon wine, but I will not drink strong wines. Mean wines, as wines of Gascony, French wines is good with meats, specially claret wine. All sweet wines and grass wines doth make a man fat.

Andrew Borde (c1490-1549) *The Breviary of Diet*

An early example of the W C Fields philosophy. When Fields was asked why he never drank water he simply replied, 'Fish fuck in it.'

Gascony is now more famous for its Armagnacs than its wines, but there are many wine makers as well producing inexpensive wines in a wide variety of styles. Try Côtes du Frontonnais AOC.

Inscription on Byron's drinking cup
made from a skull

Start not, nor deem my spirit fled:
In me behold the only skull
From which, unlike a living head,
Whatever flows is never dull.

I lived, I loved, I quaff'd like thee:
I died: let earth my bones resign:
Fill up – thou canst not injure me,
The worm hath fouler lips than thine.

Better to hold the sparkling grape,
Than nurse the earthworm's slimy brood;
And circle in the goblet's shape
The drink of gods, than reptile's food.

Where once my wit, perchance, hath shone,
In aid of others let me shine;
And when, alas! our brains are gone,
What nobler substitute than wine?

Quaff while thou canst, another race
When thou and thine, like me, are sped,
May rescue thee from earth's embrace,
And rhyme and revel with the dead.

Why not? since through life's little day
Our heads such sad effects produce?
Redeemed from worm and wasting clay,
This chance is theirs – to be of use.

George Gordon, Lord Byron 1788-1824

The image of a man sipping champagne from some elegant
lady's footwear is well known. Though where it originated

I'd be fascinated to know – some wild Christmas party at Freeman Hardy and Willis?

But what do you drink from a skull? The thought of red wine makes me slightly squeamish, so try something white and unchallenging: a glass of Frascati from central Italy. This is not a wine that the experts have any time for, but I've found on a hot summer's day, well chilled and sipped from skull or glass, it's rather delicious.

Hock cannot be too much, claret cannot be too little, iced. Indeed, I have my doubts whether any red wine should ever see the ice-pail at all. Burgundy, unquestionably, never should; and I am inclined to think, that with regard to hermitage, claret, &c., it is *always* quite sufficient to wrap a wet towel (or perhaps a wisp of wet straw is better still) about the bottle, and put it in the draught of a shady window for a couple of hours before enjoyment. I do not mention port, because that is a winter wine.

Sir Morgan O'Doherty, Bart *Maxims*

Ah, those were the days when a wisp of wet straw was as easily available as a packet of frozen peas is today.

The only red wines I enjoy slightly chilled are the red wines made by some of the most famous masters of white Burgundies. Try red Meursault; you're in for a treat.

The advice that I frequently give to young men is: don't begin drinking at all until you are seventeen or eighteen, for you are not old enough to appreciate what will be given to you. Drink only wine, beer and cider until you are thirty, and keep the reinforcement of spirits for a time when your system may be glad of such assistance. And even in your first stage never drink for the mere sake of drinking, and *never* drink with the intention of getting tipsy. A glass or two of wine will make the heart beat a little faster and will promote a sense of good humour and jollity. But to think that because two glasses produce ten degrees of gaiety four glasses will produce twenty degrees is a great delusion. People vary as to the ration of wine that is good for them, and as soon as they take more than is good for them the effect is bad, as it is if they take too much beef or bread or tea or milk. Therefore, it is important to learn as early as possible what one's proper ration is; learn it, and do not exceed it. But mark: the ration appropriate to a solitary meal will be smaller than that suitable at a party; I fancy that the gaiety of a party has an effect upon the system and makes it capable of dealing with larger quantities. I know that I should very rarely feel inclined to drink more than one half-bottle of Claret if I were dining alone; but if there were two of us I would always decant at least a bottle and a half, and possibly two bottles, and I would certainly have two bottles amongst three, and, I think, three bottles amongst four. Another peculiarity about one's appropriate ration is that it alters according to latitude. My half-bottle in London becomes a bottle in Paris; and I should not care to deny that it might double itself again in Bordeaux.

Another rule I try to teach my young friends is to eschew the cocktail before drinking wine. I am no confirmed enemy of the cocktail; there are occasions when it not only pleases but also fulfils the useful purpose of giving a tired man a fillip before he meets his guests. But even then I would choose something like a 'Sidecar', made of equal quantities of Brandy, Cointreau and lemon-juice; because the spirit is a wine spirit, and will not quarrel with the wine as Gin or Whiskey would. A Champagne cocktail is still less objectionable; only the bitters call for a rebuke. But all cocktails with spirits in them are subject to this criticism: they attack the walls of the digestive tract too violently, and partially paralyse the functions of that tract. If you have a tender spot on your skin, a scratch, for example, try the difference of spilling a little wine on it and spilling a little Brandy. Note the sharp sting of the spirit. Now try this experiment. Take one of each of two different kinds of chocolate from a mixed box, taste them, and observe the marked contrast in their tastes. Then take a sip of Brandy, roll it around your mouth, and immediately take another pair of chocolates. You will find that the difference between them is much less marked. The taste nerves are drunk; they are not doing their job. For which reason it is madness to take spirits before a meal at which delicate wine is going to be served. To a lesser degree the same criticism may be levelled at any very strong-flavoured preface to the wine; the flavour will not paralyse the taste nerves, but it will tire

them; and these strong flavours have a habit of revisiting the palate at a moment when their presence is most undesirable.

Another tip to the neophyte is, don't waste your good wines. If you are going to drink wine every day, and in this country beer is a more natural daily beverage, let your daily wine be an *ordinaire;* most wine merchants ship a sound Claret or white wine at about half a crown a bottle or one-and-six a half-bottle that should be quite good enough for daily requirements. But when a friend is coming in have something better for him. No need to give him Montrachet or Château Cheval Blanc 1921; for the ordinary dinner young men exchange the wine need not and should not cost more than 4s. a bottle. For the really great occasions bring out the bottles from behind the faggots. On these be lavish; you are trying to celebrate a notable occasion, and don't spoil the ship for the want of a ha'porth of tar. But even here a half-sovereign should get you something sufficiently outstanding. I mention these prices because if you look through the catalogues of several wine merchants you will find offered some rare and costly bottles for which you will be asked to pay anything up to three or even four hundred shillings a dozen. I do not think that at the moment of writing I could buy Château Cheval Blanc 1921 for less than 30s. a bottle, or Château Yquem 1921 for less than £1. Yet I know of one cellar in London that stables hundreds of these White Horses and also shelters hundreds of the Yquem. But the owner is a very rich man, who is expected to offer gold and myrrh and frankincense to his guests; and if he produced mere ten-shilling bottles his commercial credit would probably suffer! It is right for such people to offer their guests treasures that they can afford; but it is both foolish and unnecessary for other people to do so. Incidentally, it is in the pages devoted to Hocks that you will find the most fantastic prices quoted; and no German wine is worth such prices.

On occasions of elaboration, be careful to serve your wine against an appropriate food; but when dining alone or intimately do not take too much trouble. The theory that you cannot enjoy a Claret with fish is perfectly sound when you are drinking something like Château Ausone 1899, which Monsieur Boulestin once found his guests attempting to drink against sardines! But I never find anything to regret when I pour a little bourgeois Claret to accompany a bit of sole, or even salmon. Few strongly flavoured foods make a good background for red wine, and sweets of any sort destroy it. On the other hand, cheese and mushrooms make so good a foundation that they will even redeem an accompaniment otherwise inappropriate. Eggs are undesirable on account of their sulphur; but an omelette made with cheese or mushrooms will help a Claret right cheerfully. White wines are less exclusive in their companionship, although I never enjoy them with meat or even chicken. And I never know how best to serve the greater Hocks (when I am lucky enough to possess any!) for they seem to me to be wasted on the fish, not virile enough for the entrée or roast, and too austere for the sweets or dessert. They fall between two stools; Montrachet or a good Chablis or even a Meursault defeats them in the lists of dryness, while in a contest of sweet wines Yquem and its supporting Sauternes canter easily home ahead of a breathless Schloss Johannisberg or Ruppertsberg. Once a Hock stood me in good stead. I was showing off a cook before a good friend of mine who was a gourmet and about to pension off his own chef. My candidate prepared a menu calculated to exhibit his own skill, but taking no forethought as to how my cellar could support it. The Clarets had finished with an 1879 Château Latour, drunk with a saddle of mutton; there followed a 'Halali' salad, a delightful compound of the white meat of chicken, mushrooms, pineapple and other things, rather rich and sweet, yet not quite a sweet. This was to be followed by a Pêche Melba, with which we were to drink a bottle of Yquem 1921 . The problem was what to serve with the salad. A bottle of Ruppertsberger Hoheberg (Riesling Auslese) 1921 did the trick to perfection; sweet enough to match the pineapple in the salad, it led up to the sweeter Sauternes with a self-effacing chivalry that one does not often associate with its race. It is one of my pleasantest memories of the Rhine wines.

There are simple rules, made, like all rules, to be broken in the proper circumstances, which govern the serving of wine. Sherry is the best wine with which to open a meal; a very dry glass in the ante-room can be succeeded by one less dry with the soup. Madeira competes with Sherry as an *apéritif,* and also as a soup-squire, but, unless the Madeira is unusually good, in which case its proper place would be at dessert, I prefer Sherry. These wines may be drunk with oysters, but I prefer a still unfortified white wine – a

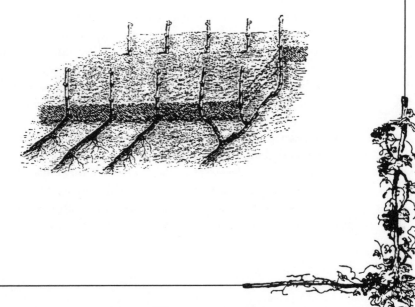

Chablis or a good Pouilly, or a Champagne, although I think the sparkle does not suit the oyster: it irritates his last moments when he is sacrificing himself for our enjoyment and deserves our consideration. By the way, I ought to have mentioned Chambéry as an agreeable *apéritif,* which is not as widely known as it might be.

With the removal of the soup the serious business begins. If it is a Champagne dinner, that wine may be served right through the meal; but for Heaven's sake do not follow it with Port. No two wines disagree more certainly or persistently than these; and yet it was Soult, and not Lannes, the gallant Duc de Montebello, that carried war into the country around Oporto. If Champagne is not to be the wine of the evening, a glass of it with the fish will not be out of place, and it will set tongues wagging more speedily than any other wine; but something less plutocratic will match the fish equally well and less ostentatiously. My preference is for white Burgundies or Rhône wines, or something from the Loire, or even a good white Rioja (I have drunk excellent Riojas, procured at very little cost). Certainly not a Sauternes or Barsac, though there is a school of thought that supports their use; and you may give the Graves to my neighbour.

The entrée will introduce your red wines; Claret before Burgundy, and a light wine before a fuller one, except that youth precedes age, a delicate old Claret setting a crown on any feast. Give your white wines half an hour in the refrigerator before serving them; bring your red wines up to the room in which they are to be drunk (or even one slightly warmer, like the cooler corners of the kitchen) about twenty-four hours before decanting them. Never warm them, either by setting them in front of the fire or by giving them a warm bath. Wine is a live thing, and sudden changes of temperature are very harmful to its flavour and bouquet. Sherry, being a white wine, comes within the icing rule; it should be served very cool; but Madeira appeals to me more if served as a red wine, *chambré,* no more.

Port is an English tradition. Port should never be served at a dinner where Sauternes is offered with the dessert; the wines kill one another. Port drinks at its best when October has settled in, and the only merit I have ever found in an east wind is the marvellous effect it has in making this wine more grateful and comforting. Port enjoys in this country the reverence more properly due to Claret; for in praising a fine bottle of Claret you are giving glory to God, but Port, under God, owes much of its excellence to the skill of its shipper. But I should be sorry to discourage the reverence accorded to Port in places where Tradition still holds sway. Many an honest drinker, bred upon Port, has felt his way towards Claret, and has died in the true faith. So drink your Port without smoking; eat a Cox's Orange Pippin or any good, firm, sweet apple with it, or crack a few nuts, if your dentist still maintains your own teeth for you; and has not fitted you with a plate to catch every pip and stone and fragment of nut that can be stowed in so limited a space.

Whether the wines conclude with Port or Sauternes or an old Claret or Burgundy, follow them with nothing but good vintage Brandy.

Maurice Healy *Stay Me With Flagons,* 1940, 1963

Well, that's pretty comprehensive, the only disagreement I would have with Mr Healy is his dislike of port after champagne. I rather enjoy the sharp contrast and unlike Cognac it doesn't wipe out all that has gone before.

If only one could buy Château d'Yquem at £1 nowadays. This is undoubtedly one of the great wines, but horrendously expensive. So to suggest sipping away at a glass whilst reading is gross indulgence, but I can think of nothing better.

He fetch'd me gifts of varied excellence;
Seven talents of fine gold; a book all framed
Of massy silver; but his gift most famed
Was twelve great vessels, fill'd with such rich wine,
As was incorruptible and divine.
He kept it as his jewel, which none knew
But he himself, his wife, and he that drew.
It was so strong, that never any fill'd
A cup, where that was but by drops instilled,
And drunk it off, but 'twas before allay'd
With twenty parts water; yet so sway'd
The spirit of that little, that the whole
A sacred odour breath'd about the bowl;
Had you the odour smelt, and scent it cast,
It would have vexed you to forbear the taste.
But then, the taste gain'd too, the spirit it brought
To dare things high, set up on end my thought.

George Chapman from his translation of Homer's *Odyssey*, 1614–15

This is probably the earliest known record of a winemaking kit – you can buy them at Boots now. The major part of such kits, even today, is a vessel of grape concentrate – just add water and Hey Homer.

Try a glass of good fruity Alsace.

The wine was excellent: the Port was of some famous vintage, I forget which; the Madeira was forty years old; the Claret was a present from Bordeaux. As a matter of course, we talked wine. No company of Englishmen can assemble together for an evening without doing that. Every man in this country who is rich enough to pay income-tax, has, at one time or other of his life, effected a very remarkable transaction in wine. Sometimes he has made such a bargain as he never expects to make again. Sometimes he is the only man in England, not a peer of the realm, who has got a single drop of a certain famous vintage which has perished from the face of the earth. Sometimes he has purchased, with a friend, a few last left dozens from the cellar of a deceased potentate, at a price so exorbitant that he can only wag his head and decline mentioning it – and, if you ask his friend, that friend will wag his head and decline mentioning it also. Sometimes he has been at an out-of-the-way country inn; has found the Sherry not drinkable; has asked if there is no other wine in the house; has been informed that there is some 'sourish foreign stuff that nobody ever drinks' has called for a bottle of it; has found it Burgundy, such as all France cannot now produce; has cunningly kept his own counsel with the widowed landlady, and has bought the whole stock for 'an old song'. Sometimes he knows the proprietor of a famous tavern in London; and he recommends his one or two particular friends, the next time they are passing that way, to go in and dine, and give his compliments to the landlord, and ask for a bottle of the brown Sherry, with the light blue – as distinguished from the dark blue – seal. Thousands of people dine there every year, and think they have got the famous Sherry when they get the dark blue seal; but – and, by no means let it go any further – the real wine, the famous wine, is the light blue seal; and nobody in England knows it but the landlord and his friends. In all these wine conversations, whatever variety there may be in the various experiences related, one of two great first principles is invariably assumed by each speaker in succession. Either he knows more about it than anyone else – or he has got better wine of his own even than the excellent wine he is now drinking. Men can get together sometimes without talking of women, without talking of horses, without talking of politics; but they cannot assemble to eat a meal together without talking of wine; and they cannot talk of wine without assuming to each one of themselves an absolute infallibility in connexion with that single subject, which they would shrink from asserting in relation to any other topic under the sun.

from *Household Words* (1850-9)

Oh dear, the writer is absolutely bang on. I myself have boasted of buying seventeen magnums of 1982 Dom Pérignon at £50 per magnum on countless occasions and here I am doing it again.

To take away the taste of wine snobbery, half a pint of best bitter.

'Hocks, too have compassed age. I have tasted senior hocks. Their flavours are as a brook of many voices: they have depth also. Senatorial Port! we say. We cannot say that of any other wine. Port is deep-sea deep. It is in its flavour deep; mark the difference. It is like a classic tragedy, organic in conception. An ancient Hermitage has the light of the antique; the merit that it can grow to an extreme old age; a merit. Neither of Hermitage nor of Hock can you say that it is the blood of those long years, retaining the strength of youth with the wisdom of age. To Port for that! Port is our noblest legacy! Observe, I do not compare the wines: I distinguish the qualities. Let them live together for our enrichment; they are not rivals like the Idean three. Were they rivals, a fourth would challenge them. Burgundy has great genius. It does wonders within its period; it does all except to keep up in the race; it is short lived. An aged Burgundy runs with a beardless Port. I cherish the fancy that Port speaks the sentences of wisdom. Burgundy sings the inspired ode. Or put it, that Port is the Homeric hexameter, Burgundy the Pindaric dithyramb. What do you say?'

'The comparison is excellent, sir.'

'The distinction, you should remark. Pindar astounds. But his elder brings us the more sustaining cup. One is a fountain of prodigious assent. One is the unsounded purple sea of marching billows.'

George Meredith *The Egoist*, 1879

It's rather comforting to know that wine snobs are nothing new. Which would you rather drink, the Homeric hexameter or the Pindaric dithyramb?

Let's go for the dithyramb – a glass of Saint-Véran from the Mâconnais-Beaujolais border.

In 1970 Arthur Marshall set a competition on wine snobbery in a wine magazine. This is part of A G Cairns Smith's entry.

A: What's the grape do you think? *Kabinet Semolina?*

B: Possibly, although are we not too far south for that? More likely a *Pompidou Noir.*

A: But surely we're north of the river?

B: . . . but south of the petrol station . . .

A: . . . but facing *east* on that slope between Henri's bistro and the cross-roads.

B: Even so, until Jean-Jacques went down with his *foie troublé* most of this wine was made from the vines beside the *abattoir* – which were, of course, pre-haemophilia *pompidous.*

A: (suddenly) Have another look now: I think the wine is trying to tell us something (swill swill, sniff sniff, gurgle gurgle, gargle, cough, splutter, choke . . .)
(A falls to the floor. His face assumes the colour of a *cru supérieur Châteauneuf-du-Pape* in an off year. He expires.)

B: (Sniffing with great concentration) Yes, *Pompidou Noir*, definitely.

Wine Mine

Let this be a warning to us all especially when tasting is combined with quaffing.

Something sobering is required, a glass of Perrier with a twist of lemon perhaps?

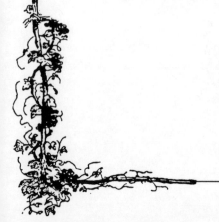

Now anyone who thinks that a vivid appreciation of the exquisite flavours of wine and food implies greed, is the victim of confused thinking. Taste is one of the five senses, and the man who tells us with priggish pride that he does not care what he eats is merely boasting of his sad deficiency: he might as well be proud of being deaf or blind, or, owing to a perpetual cold in the head, of being devoid of the sense of smell. There is no reason to suppose that taste is in any way a lower sense than the other four; a fine palate is as much a gift as an eye that discerns beauty, or an ear that appreciates and enjoys subtle harmonies of sound, and we are quite right to value the pleasures that all our senses give us and educate their perceptions. The greedy man is he who habitually eats too much, knowing that he is injuring his bodily health thereby, and this is a vice to which not the *gourmet* but the *gourmand* is a slave. But Mr Harry, though he undoubtedly was a *gourmand* also, and ate prodigious quantities of food, could not, so admirable was his digestion, and so well large masses of solid food suited him, be called greedy at all. He had a noble and healthy appetite, *le foie du charbonnier*, and as he once observed with a very proper satisfaction,

'I should like to see my stomach disagree with anything I choose to give it.'

E F Benson *As We Were*, 1930

The lack of importance we give to taste in this country is really quite shocking. Just when our cuisine is reaching new heights, when the availability of good and reasonably priced wines has never been greater, we have to face the daunting enemy of fast food. Here in the UK we do nothing about it. In France they have realized the threat fast food poses not only to their culture but to the fast food generation's enjoyment of life and they're fighting back. In French schools children as young as six are given regular lessons in taste to educate their palates, so that when they eat their burgers etc., which of course they must, they will at least appreciate that there is an alternative. If we don't do anything about this in this country we may be in danger in generations to come of producing a society in which good food and wine are so alien, so strange to the palate, that they are beyond enjoyment.

Well, that's got that out of my system! Let's give Mr Harry's stomach a robust red, a glass of Hermitage, the wonderfully round and deep wine of the Northern Rhône.

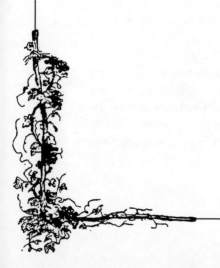

Every year on 26 December, The Waterside Inn closes its doors for a good six weeks and my wife and I crawl onto a jet plane and head towards a destination which will soothe the aching body and scattered brain. The first few days are mute, so there is always the search for the pleasure of the palate to cover those silences over dinner.

In 1988, Robyn and I set out for Sydney on a direct flight. Normally we break the flight, but for her family reasons we had to be there straight away. We always go straight to Palm Beach, about 45 minutes from Sydney. I love it there. The air is sweet, the breeze gentle and, because most of our friends have already been summering themselves in lethargy for some weeks, they are soothing and kind. Before leaving Bray, I telephoned a friend called Michael McMahon, who at the time owned a restaurant called Barrenjoey House in Palm Beach. 'Michael,' I said, 'nous sommes en route, command les Mud Crabs, the rest of the menu is up to you.' Michel's reply is unprintable, but in good Aussie fashion, he replied 'She'll be right.'

We arrived bruised, tired, jetlagged and generally in a condition of 'too far gone . . . terminal!' Our friend, seeing our condition, thought it prudent to keep his distance. As we settled into our canvas chairs under the palm trees, a glass of chilled white was poured and the vocal cords muttered 'delicious, give me more.' We were drinking a Petaluma Rhine Riesling, from South Australia, which was fruity, crisp and a delicious hit to the palate. Then arrived an enormous white porcelain bowl groaning with Mud Crab, with the steam rising and the aroma pervading the warm air. I broke one of the claws and decided that should my call from the almighty be at that second, he would have to wait until I had finished the bowl. The flesh was so sweet, moist and rich; the meat falls in chunks, satisfying the palate and yet driving one crazy for another mouthful. Our hands, our faces, our glasses were covered with our greedy pleasure.

Another porcelain bowl appeared with lemon, hot water and white towels for bathing. We had now managed to string a few words together which almost resembled a sentence. A small plate of crab meat was placed in front of us . With the work done for us and the effect of the Riesling, I truly thought I was in fact going to survive the day. The crab meat had been lightly marinated in lime juice, and garnished with sun-dried tomatoes. Another South Australian wine in the shape of a bottle of Mount Adam Chardonnay arrived . . . . What is next, I thought, fish? No, it was yet more Mud Crab sautéed with a touch of lemon grass, a hint of chilli and soya sauce. The depth of this Chardonnay, which I believe to be the best in Australia, was a perfect foil for the aromatics of this dish.

To that evening and since I have never been able to eat the same product, three times in one meal. It is against everything I believe in terms of a balance of ingredients. The challenge was still out of course because there was dessert to come. Michael finally left the white flag flying and came to join us. I am not a man known to lose his words, especially after a stunning meal. I was so soporific by this time, I could barely stop the tears of a man returned from the dead.

To complete this wonderful over-indulgence of Mud Crab, we finished with a perfect white peach which was so sweet in its natural state, I felt the only complement to it was to pour a little of the 1979 Bollinger RD, which Michael had so thoughtfully arrived with, to celebrate the return of the power of speech.

Michel Roux, quoted in Derek Nimmo (ed) *Memorable Dinners*, 1991

How pleasing to find a great chef writing about the food of another continent with such evident enthusiasm and pleasure.

Michel Roux's tribute to the wines sets the taste buds going too. Here he extols the white wines, so may I suggest a red to illustrate the depth and range of South Australian wines. The small family-run winery of Hollick produces Ravenswood Cabernet Sauvignon which my wine merchant, Trevor Hughes, describes, in glowing terms as 'Surely a New World Classic'. Try it and judge for yourself.

The Wine Connoisseur

The Wine Connoisseur is one who knows good wine from bad and who appreciates the distinctive merits of different wines.

The Wine Connoisseur drinks wine in moderation, but regularly and appreciatively. It is excess – not habit – which blunts appreciation.

A little wine every day costs very little money and is the safest, as well as the pleasantest, tonic for body and mind alike. But wine, whatever its name, its age or its cost, must be honest if it is to be good and to do good.

How can you tell good wine from bad; how can you become a Wine Connoisseur?

By using your senses and your common sense. By looking at it, smelling it and tasting it with critical eyes, nose and palate before committing it to your veins and your brain.

Look at your wine critically: it must be not only clear but brilliant, be a ruby or amber, young or old, cheap or dear. If it be dull or thick, reject it; if bright, let it go before the tribunal of your nose.

Smell your wine critically: it must be clean-smelling. If you can detect the slightest mouldy, foul smell, or some unnatural, artificial scent, however, faint, leave it alone. If its discreet aroma is pleasant, remain a while with bowed head over your glass; try to remember the occasion when you last met the same charming 'bouquet' and what was the name of the wine.

Then you may send your wine to the next court where your palate awaits it.

Taste your wine critically: it must be clean and pleasant. If you detect any unsavoury, sour or merely suspicious taste, spit it out as you would a bad oyster or a piece of tainted meat. But if the wreath of tiny taste-buds of your tongue and palate receive your wine joyfully, pause but one instant, again to search your memory for the name and vintage of the wine you are drinking, and then swallow it gratefully.

André Simon *A Wine Primer*, 1940

Indisputably one of the great wine writers, no pretensions and a gentle stripping away of mystique, admirable.

This time a great white Burgundy, Chevalier Montrachet.

In July 1986 I received a very puzzling invitation. The time and place were clear enough. I was bid for 11 a.m. on 30 September to Château d'Yquem, indisputably the greatest property in Sauternes, the sweet wine district south-east of Bordeaux. The host was quite plain too: Herr Hardy Rodenstock, perhaps the most famous of a new group of near-fanatical fine wine collectors in Germany. But *what* exactly was I being invited to?

In the English part of the trilingual invitation, it was described simply as a 'wine tasting with rare wines' which 'will end at about 10 p.m.' I was told to wear a metaphorical black tie, that my invitation was for one person only and was not transferable, and that I should reply, by registered post, by 30 August. I reckoned that any event to which a typical German postman should not be relied upon to convey my acceptance would probably be worth going to. I was right.

The 'wine tasting with rare wines' turned out to be a twelve-course meal to which forty of us sat down at about noon on Tuesday and from which we got up at one o'clock on Wednesday morning. We were each served *sixty-six* different wines, not to taste – that would have been easy – but to *drink*. There was not a spittoon in sight, until about eight o'clock in the evening when Michael Broadbent (under whose hammer a good proportion of all that we enjoyed must have passed a time or two) finally secured a rather grand-looking *cache-pot* for himself and his neighbours. Around 3500 splinter-stemmed crystal glasses were, in sobering progression, cleaned, filled, emptied, and cleaned again. . . .

A flight of four German wines was served first, including a Beerenauslese Trocken, if you please (a 'sweet dry' curiosity since banned by the German authorities), with a 'simple' salad of red mullet, artichokes and potatoes.

The *cassolette de homard aux perles de légumes* was temptingly rich for the second of a dozen courses, but the four white burgundies served with it were utterly distracting – particularly a rivetingly pure brace of Bienvenue Bâtard-Montrachets, 1979 and 1982, from André Ramonet.

Our sixteen Ygrecs followed with two more fish courses and suggested conclusively to me that this dry wine does not improve with more than ten years in bottle, but they served admirably to heighten the high point of this day-long succession of high points,

a run of five vintages of Chateau d'Yquem, the sweet wine and no messing, that marked the end of our first session at the table. Before our sliver of fresh *foie gras* sautéed with white grapes and Yquem 1976 (it's no good describing wines as '76 in a Hardy context), we were to taste Yquem 1858, 1847, 1811 and one amazing bottle that had been put at about 1750.

Hardy, who has never disclosed exactly how or where in Paris he unearthed the Thomas Jefferson bottles, had heard that there were still some treasures from the former Tsars' cellars to be found in Leningrad. Yquem had long been a favourite with the Russian court, the Tsar having paid 20,000 gold francs for a barrel of Yquem in 1847 in one well-documented transaction. He managed to find this bottle, flask-shaped and deep indigo-coloured glass engraved all over with tiny white-painted flowers, grapes and vine leaves, as was the custom then, and marked with the arms of the Sauvage family (who did not transfer ownership of Yquem by marriage into the Lur-Saluces family till 1785).

Analysis of the glass, once Hardy had somehow spirited the bottle out of the USSR, suggested that it was mid-eighteenth century, making this wine that we were about to taste the oldest that had probably ever been tasted from a bottle. (Great sweet white wines probably stand a better chance of survival over a few hundred years than most, and several of those present had drooled over a Thomas Jefferson bottle of Yquem 1784 at the previous year's event in Germany.)

But first we had to eat our bread and butter – and what bread and butter! The nineteenth-century Yquems, culled from cellars as far apart as Scotland and Venezuela, had turned deep tawny as very old white wines are wont to do, but tasted by no means over the hill. The 1858 was starting to be a little aggressive and the 1811 was perhaps a bit attenuated, but the 1874 was absolutely great wine, utterly alive and kicking, very vigorous, round and rich with good acid balance and a lovely long, well-integrated flavour that just went on and on.

Silence fell as the young sommelier imported from Munich tapped away at the most ancient bottle of all. Then came a communal squeal of delight as the cork emerged intact, only to crumble immediately, exhausted by the effort of preserving this wine so long. There was just one bottle, which everyone wanted to touch, enough for a good-sized glass for each of the four tables. When it was poured, it looked almost like claret, so deep-coloured and red was it. The temptation was to admire and comment, but Michael Broadbent, with the natural sense of slightly bossy responsibility that has got him where he is, reminded us sharply that this was very old wine that should be tasted immediately, before it faded.

There is no way four glasses, however beautiful (they were specially made and engraved for this particular wine by Riedel) can be shared elegantly by forty tasters, but somehow everyone managed to taste this extraordinary liquid: deep foxy red, creamy rich in texture, almost unctuous with a slight minerally edge, just starting to fall apart, but still very definitely a top quality, naturally sweet wine. What an experience, to think that we were tasting a wine made perhaps twenty years before Napoleon was even born.

The special glasses were duly auctioned for charity, the Count nobly setting a price of 12,000 francs for the first set of four. I felt sorry for Michael Broadbent who, after tasting thirty-odd wines, and making one of his extra-thorough notes on each, was expected to conduct the sale.

By now it was five in the afternoon and the golden autumn light was gently fading. We were all dying to get outside before it disappeared so, pausing only to savour the *foie gras* and 1976 Yquem, we trooped outside, the earnest ones for a tour of the cellars, the Brits for a quiet nap under the tree.

Now, I think you probably have some idea of how the rest of the day went by now. Yes, there was more of the same, only a little bit different. 'Standout' wines among the thirty-three that followed included Château Canon 1966 from a jeroboam and Calon-Ségur 1966 from an imperial (the equivalent of six and eight bottles respectively in one); Château Pétrus and Cheval Blanc in magnum, both 1921; a jeroboam of Château Mouton-Rothschild 1929 that, even at ten o'clock with Brillat-Savarin and *pain noir aux pruneaux*, was so sensationally complete it revived my flagging spirits; and two more absolutely gorgeous vintages of Château d'Yquem, 1937 and 1921.

The staff of the château and restaurants had behaved beautifully, with admirable manners and stamina throughout, but how about the guests? Since that day, a lot of people have asked me, some more politely than others, but weren't you all horribly *drunk?* And the answer, amazingly enough, is no. Funnily enough, for me and I suspect many others, the day turned into almost a battle for survival rather than an opportunity to maximize consumption. Although I consciously sipped rather than drank, I did find myself flushing down an Anadin with some Lanson 1964 at about eight o'clock (a practice which I'm sure should not be condoned on any basis). Next morning I felt eerily healthy, even when I got up at 6 a.m. to catch the red-eye special back to Heathrow. I did notice the in-flight breakfast wasn't up to much though.

Jancis Robinson Food and Wine Adventures, 1987

How can one follow that? You almost feel sorry for the airline cabin staff proffering their nourishing but simple fare at that early hour.

Trying to suggest a wine after such an experience seems presumptuous but for we lesser mortals a bottle of 1950 Château d'Yquem might set the right tone, but be warned, one bottle alone will set you back all of £300!

Try the Bandol, Château des Vannières 1972 CB. This red wine comes from the estate of Mme Boisseaux right on the edge of the Mediterranean. 'It has,' said Peter Reynier 'an elegant warm bouquet and leaves a delicious fresh tang on the palate. Powerful, dark and quite heady, this is a real Marlon Brando of wine.'

Katie Bourke *Decanter* (quoted in *Private Eye*, 'Pseuds Corner')

We've had wine as toothpaste now wine as actors. It's not a bad game – a bone-dry and subtle Chablis, a Joanna Lumley of a wine. A rip-roaring red, a Jack Nicholson of a wine.

To suggest anything else but Ms Bourke's Château des Vannières '72 seems devilish and 1972 was a better year for Marlon Brando than 1995.

The Man in the Moon Drinks Claret

Bacchus, the father of drunken nowles,
Full mazers, beakers, glasses, bowls,
Greasie flapdragons, flamish upsefriese,
With health's stab'd in arms upon naked knees.

Rich wine is good:
It heats the blood,
It makes an old man lusty,
The young to brawle,
And drawers up call
Before being too much musty.

Such gambles, such tricks, such figaries,
We fetch, though we touch no Canaryes;
French wine till the welkin roares,
And cry out a plague of your scores.

There is no sound
The ears can wound
As lids of wine-pots clinking;
There's no such sport when, all amort,
Men cry let's fall to drinking.

Our man in the moon drinks claret,
With powder beef, turnep, and carret;
If he doth so, why should not you
Drink wine untill the sky looks blew?

Hey for a turn thus above ground, hey!
O my noddle too heavy doth way!
Metheglin, perry, syder nor strong ale,
Are half so hevy, be they nere so stale.
Wine in our bodies can never rumble,
Down now and then though it makes us stumble;
Yet scrambling up, a drunkard feels no pain,
But cryes,—sirra, boy, tother pottle again!

We can drink no more unless we have full
    pipes of Trinidado.
Give us the best, it keeps our brains
More warm than can friezado.
It makes us sing,
And cry, hey jing,
And laugh when pipes lie broken.
For which to pay,
At going away,
We scorn a mustard token.

If, then, you do love my oast claret,
Fat powder beef, turnep, and carret,
Come agen and agen,
And still welcome, gentlemen.

William Basse (d. c.1653)

A drinking song written, if I'm not much mistaken, when the author was pretty drunk himself. Witness the desperation of some of the lyrics, 'It makes us sing/And cry, hey jing.'

There are many theories about drink and creativity. One of my favourites came from the wonderful man and great teacher who ran the Bristol Old Vic Theatre School when I was there, Nat Brenner. Quite often a group of students would be invited up to his flat on top of the school at the end of the day and there we would sit and talk about the theatre until late at night, while drinking far too much Guinness and smoking endless cigarettes. One night as we were about to leave the smoke-filled living room, Nat got up, stretched and said, 'I don't think Shakespeare drank much, certainly not when he was writing. It's all too polished to perfection.

'Now Ben Jonson drank. I think he spent most of his day drinking. He'd come home pretty pissed and go to bed. But he always made sure that by his bed were paper, ink, quill and candle, because when he got up to pee in the night, which he must have had to do often, that's when the Muse must have struck. "That's a bloody good idea," he'd think and sit on the bed to write.'

I'm sure there's some essential truth to the theory. To this day, if someone mentions Jonson the image of the man sitting in flickering candle-light in a state between drunkenness and hangover, dashing off his plays, comes straight into my mind's eye.

To Bordeaux, a glass or more of Château Caronne-Sainte-Gemme.

The parishes in which are the most celebrated vineyards are Margaux, Pauillac, St Jullien, St Estèphe, Listrac, St Laurent, St Seurin de Cadourne, and several others.

Châteaux Lafitte, Margaux, and Latour are decidedly superior to those that rank as second growths. This is attributable, not only to their excellent positions, but almost equally to the great care bestowed to uphold their reputation, which has long enabled the proprietors to get prices much higher than their neighbours.

Demanding incessant care and attention in every way, one of the most anxious and difficult parts is to have a good combination of vines; for no more in the vegetable than in the animal world can a successful result be derived from only one stock, however pure and perfect this stock at first may be. One vine gives delicacy, another body, another flavour; and the grapes from those and two or three more, with other characteristics, produce wine superior to any that could be got from any one kind.

But it is not always that these first growths are superior to the second, for occasionally the latter, and even third growths, prove better. The St Emilions are fuller and stouter, and have a deeper colour, than the Médocs; and, although less delicate and fine, have a very agreeable taste, and are generally much liked. The Vins de Graves are also favourites, though not equal to the Médocs. The parishes which produce the best wines of this class are Talence, Pessac, Mérignac, Léognan. The Vins de Côtes, Blaye, &c., though deficient in flavour, and not to be compared to many of the Médocs, when of a good year, are very pleasant, and are much used in Bordeaux.

I remember, when dining a few years ago with a friend at an inn in the village of Margaux, within a stone's throw of the Château, we were much amused on finding the wine so very bad that we could drink it only with water.

When in Bordeaux, a few months back, I tasted Château Lafitte 1858, which could not be bought for less than 100*l.*, and the same growth of 1860, which could be had for 5*l.* per hogshead.

This proves what I have stated, and if wine-merchants will go over themselves to select according to their judgement and the opinion of respectable brokers or merchants, they should mention no name at all, but describe clearly what is wanted, with the limit of price. It is certainly more satisfactory to go to the place, to taste and compare the contents of various cellars; but, unless there be a knowledge of the language of the country, the tasting and comparison must be confined to the cellars of the few houses who are in the habit of dealing with England (and not even in London are there more highly respectable merchants). Yet they have long been accustomed to prices and profits very different from many equally respectable French houses, who possess as good wine, and have not been allowed by their native fellow-dealers to get habituated to such gains.

Thomas George Shaw *The Wine, the Vine and the Cellar*, 1863

Here is an example of the extraordinary care the top growers give to their finest vines. Today I'm happy to say there are more and more producers taking real trouble with their wines from vine to bottle. The result is an explosion of good wines at all prices, sometimes from areas that even ten years ago you wouldn't have known produced such quality.

It's also an interesting nineteenth-century warning of the fat-cat English wine merchants. Happily again with the ease with which one can travel to France and the lifting of Customs limits for personal consumption, I don't think many wine merchants charging high prices with little expertise survive.

You can't mention Lafite, Margaux and Latour and not try some (this is becoming a very expensive read). So a glass of Château Lafite.

Château Latour 1930. I heard the maître say, 'It's like old lace', and Clive Gibson likening it to the music of Clementi, and I understood what they meant. I was not enjoying the taste of an excellent claret, I had discovered a new level of appreciation, a new form of communication for me, the communication which this wine demands is exactly the same as that which you get from great music or great poetry.

Lord Snowdon Vogue (quoted in Private Eye 'Pseuds Corner')

This was printed, unkindly I think, in 'Pseuds Corner' in *Private Eye*. The maître's description of the wine as 'old lace' is wonderful and Snowdon's description of his feelings seems to me entirely justified.

Well, it's got to be a visit to the bank manager and a bottle of Château Latour. If you can get hold of a bottle of 1930, I want to know!

The wines of Bordeaux first attained their reputation through the following incident:

The Duke de Richelieu having been named governor of the province, on his arrival at his post the principal inhabitants went to pay him their compliments, and presented him some wine of their growth. The Duke, who was an excellent judge of wine, tasted it at first from mere politeness, but afterwards because he liked it. On his return to Paris, being invited to sup with King Louis XV, he requested permission to introduce to his Majesty one of the dignitaries of his province, and accordingly presented to the King an old bottle well covered with cobwebs and dust. His Majesty smiled, tasted the wine, and declared it to be some of the best he had ever drunk. From that day, or rather than night, the fortune of the Bordelais was made.

Charles Tovey *Wit, Wisdom and Morals: Distilled from Bacchus*, 1878

Well, I never. You live and learn – and then you die and forget it all.
A bottle of Château Coufran from the Haut-Médoc.

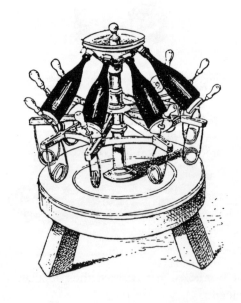

Drinking Song

She tells me with claret she cannot agree,
And she thinks of a hogshead whene'er she sees me;
For I smell like a beast, and therefore must I
Resolve to forsake her, or claret deny.
Must I leave my dear bottle, that was always my friend,
And I hope will continue so to my life's end?
Must I leave it for her? 'Tis a very hard task:
Let her go to the devil! – bring the other full flask.

Had she taxed me with gaming, and bid me forbear,
'Tis a thousand to one I had lent her an ear:
Had she found out my Sally, up three pair of stairs,
I had balked her, and gone to St James's to prayers.
Had she bade me read homilies three times a day,
She perhaps had been humoured with little to say;
But, at night, to deny me my bottle of red,
Let her go to the devil! – there's no more to be said.

Anonymous

I find this rather sad. There's nothing wrong with the author's consumption; a bottle a day is reasonable. But the fact that he realizes he couldn't be without it I find alarming. Alcoholism is not to do with quantity but reliance. So I suggest a couple of days' abstinence from the grape. If you find this at all difficult – beware.

It is related of Mr Alderman Faulkner, of convivial memory, that one night, when he expected his guests to sit late and try the strength of his Claret and his head, he took the precaution to place in his wine glass a strawberry, which his doctor, he said, had recommended to him on account of its cooling qualities. On the faith of this specific, he drank even more deeply, and, as might be expected, was carried away earlier than usual. When some of his friends condoled with him next day, and attributed his misfortune to six bottles of Claret which he had drunk, the alderman was extremely indignant: 'The Claret,' he said, 'was sound, and never could do anybody any harm' – his discomfiture was altogether caused by 'that confounded single strawberry' which he had kept all night at the bottom of his glass.

Charles Tovey *Wit, Wisdom and Morals: Distilled from Bacchus*, 1878

I didn't expect to be discussing the merits or otherwise of soft fruits in a book about wine. Of course, if Alderman Faulkner is right, we should watch our strawberry consumption carefully lest we too, having enjoyed a bowl too many, are 'carried away earlier than usual' and have to spend the next day in bed drinking claret to recover.

Try some Château Meyney from St Estèphe.

12 February 1964: I was staying with Philippe and Pauline de Rothschild at Château Mouton. John Huston was staying there too. I was writing the script of a film which he was directing. It was a spring-like day, warm and still. In the morning I had worked with Philippe on my translations of some poems he had written, and afterwards I walked through the vineyards with John Huston as far as Château Lafite, talking about the film. There was another walk in the afternoon when Philippe and Pauline joined us. 'The sun set red,' my diary says, 'and the air was cold.'

Dinner that night was in Petit Mouton – meals were taken in one or other of the two houses as Pauline decided. I don't know why I didn't keep the menu; I had done so on two other days, February the 9th and 10th. On the 10th the diary says: 'after the excellent 1921 claret came the really extraordinary Mouton Rothschild 1870, six years from achieving its century, which surpassed any wine I had ever drunk before.' But February the 12th also has its place in my memory. John Huston was born in 1906. I was born in 1907. Our birth year wines were brought from the cellars. The 1906 almost rivalled the 1870. It accompanied the meal as Ariel partnered Prospero – 'dearly, my delicate Ariel'. But my year was judged to be a poor bottle and was sent away from the table, to be replaced (as we all are) by a younger wine, 1953, Coronation year.

Was it on one of these three February days, or on a return visit to Mouton later in the year, that the Swiss ambassador, when talking about the English theatre, mentioned several times someone called Clarence Tarragon? It took me a little while to realize that he was a man I called Terence Rattigan.

The nearest I came to my own birth year had already been drunk on February the 9th, a Mouton Rothschild 1909. To celebrate my existence I give the menu for that evening's dinner:

Consommé aux moules
Cailles flambées
Purée de petit pois
Fonds d'artichauts farcis
Foie gras à la gelée
Salade
Fromages
Les trois glaces

Mercurey 1959
Mouton Rothschild 1945
Mouton Rothschild 1929
Mouton Rothschild 1909
Yquem 1949

Those vintage years cover a fair swathe of my life:

1959: I had been to America and exchanged it for Italy.
1945: I began writing a play in peacetime.
1929: I was midway in a three-year stint as a schoolmaster.
1909: I first went into short trousers instead of petticoats.
1949: *The Lady's not for Burning* opened in London.

Christopher Fry, quoted in Derek Nimmo (ed) *Memorable Dinners*, 1991

The oldest bottle of wine I've drunk was, like Mr Fry, a birth year bottle. It was my father's seventieth birthday and my wine merchant Trevor Hughes found me a bottle of 1915 Pommard-Rugiens. So on 13 December 1985 we drank it. There were seven of us at the table so we had little more than half a glass each. I have never before or since tasted anything that came anywhere near it. If you ever get the chance to taste good old red wine, jump at it. You need be no expert, you will simply have a taste experience you will remember for years.

We have to drink Mouton Rothschild. Don't worry about the year, just the cost.

When the soup has been removed and the fish makes its appearance Sherry has played its part, and a larger glass requires filling with a wine that can remain unperturbed by piscine flavours. Most fish are strong and pronounced in taste, and to savour a really delicate wine in their company would be impossible. Other more discreet denizens of the water may be accompanied by wines which normally would be out of place at this course; it perhaps will surprise the reader to know that it is possible to drink Claret with salmon, one of the most distinctively flavoured of fish; while sole and turbot are always well-mannered and inoffensive, and cause no wine, red or white, to leave the table. But these may be served with a sauce that perpetrates the offence that they themselves have avoided; the anchovy has a knack of turning up as an accompaniment to the most innocent sole or turbot, and so completely monopolizing the palate as to make all discrimination in the matter of wine impossible. For such occasions Heaven has allowed large quantities of white wine to be made in Bordeaux and sold under the name of 'Graves', although much of it comes from other parts of the Gironde. It certainly justifies Heywood's jest that 'none but sextons drink Graves wine'. To make it fall bright recourse is had so freely to the device of sulphuring the casks (a necessary and proper practice when performed in moderation) that each glass tastes as though it had been stirred with a lucifer match. There are well-known vineyards that owe their fame entirely to the white wines they produce; I have patiently searched out samples of their wine of a good year, duly chilled the bottle, and tried the wine as favourably as I could. I am bound to say that the distance between the best Graves and the worst Graves that I have ever drunk would require a micrometer to measure it. I make one honourable exception. It is not generally known that the great Château Haut Brion, where one of the most illustrious of Clarets is produced, also makes a small quantity of white wine. This is a true Graves, for it comes from the Graves district. And it is a very fine wine indeed: the only white wine of Bordeaux that I have ever tasted which I should venture to offer in competition with a white Burgundy. In a good year it has a bouquet that suggests Sauternes; yet it is absolutely dry. In a Soho restaurant I once heard a lady ask for 'a dry Sauternes', which then sounded to me like a remarkable contradiction in terms. For I thought of Sauternes in terms of

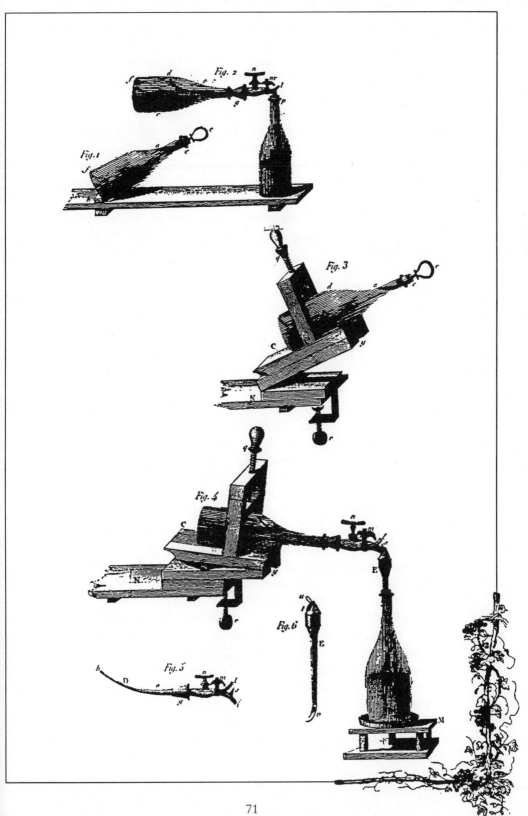

71

Château Yquem, most luscious and lovely of liquors; I had not then met the Haut Brion Blanc. Now, although the French do serve the rich Sauternes with the fish, I have always thought it a heresy; the flavours clash and destroy one another. But white Haut Brion can go very well with the fish; it pleases the nose with its rich aromatic bouquet, while the austerity of its dryness enables it to look with scorn upon the fishiest of dishes. I have even had the luck to drink vintages of this wine against one another; neither of them very great, for 1918 was not a good year for either red or white wines, and 1922 was only a little better for white than for red, for which it was very poor. But the two Haut Brions showed very prettily, and each wore its rue with a difference. Those sufficiently eccentric to desire my society will find a bottle of Haut Brion Blanc a good bait for the trap.

My rage against the average bottle of Graves arises from the thought that the soil which went to its growing might have been devoted to a red wine, wherein Bordeaux, like Sylvia, 'excels each mortal thing'. But happily there are other districts where the white wines come nearer to my palate. Of all these Burgundy is *facile princeps*. It cannot be too often proclaimed and reaffirmed that the white wines of Burgundy are as far (nay, much further) above the white wines of Bordeaux (not counting the Sauternes) as the red wines of Bordeaux are above the red wines of Burgundy. And there is such a range of them. Let us begin, in true Irish fashion, with a wine that is not, strictly speaking, a Burgundy at all: Chablis. The district whence our Chablis comes (or ought to come) is away in the north, near Auxerre; practically all the wine we know as Burgundy comes from south of Dijon, and between that town and Chablis is a long stretch of country, undistinguished by any notable vineyards. Kimmeridge in Dorset has given its name to a belt of bituminous clay that appears to dive thence beneath the Channel and to make a very limited reappearance at Auxerre. It is apparently this clay that gives the peculiar virtue to the soil of Chablis and causes the clean and delicate flavour of its wines. For Chablis is unlike the other white Burgundies, although made from the same grapes. The noble Pinot gives it its excellence, when it has it; not every bottle that cries 'Chablis! Chablis!' shall merit commendation. For, as elsewhere in Burgundy, there is a war of the vines. For centuries the Pinot has been in a sort of competition with the upstart Gamay, a vine that, like many of the base-born, can flourish where a more delicate plant would perish. Now, the Pinot will grow on the slopes around Chablis, but it declines on the lower levels, where, however, the prolific and thrusting Gamay will thrive. By the Law of Place-names of Origin, wine made in the Chablis district can be sold as Chablis, no matter of what grape it is made. But only the wine made from the Pinot is real Chablis, as a wine-lover understands the word. And, as French law does not run in England, the bottle of Chablis you get in a little Soho restaurant may not even be Gamay Chablis; it may come from one of the devil's-cauldrons where they make the wine that ignorant people drink to their harm.

Your genuine Chablis has a glint of green underlying its yellow, or so it always appears to my eye; it is as lovely to look upon as to taste. It is probably entitled to the honour of having been my first introduction to great wine; for, as I have explained, I was a teetotaller when young. And my first lapse was produced by a piece of casuistry that I almost blush to record. In the summer of 1910 I was in Francis Meynell's company when we met my own parish priest, the late Canon O'Mahony of Blackrock, known to a host of friends as 'Father O'James'. Most hospitable of men, he promptly swept us off to the Villa Villa, then at the height of its popularity and, as I discovered a few nights ago, now, alas! no more. Food was quickly provided; drink was discussed. And to my amazement the Canon, a gold badge of the League of the Cross on his watch-chain, suggested a bottle of Chianti. 'But,' said I, 'you and I are teetotallers.' He looked at me gravely, but with a twinkle in his eye. 'We took the pledge,' said he, 'for one of two purposes, that is to say, either we wished to avoid becoming drunkards or we wished to give example to others. Now, we can't give example, good or bad, here because nobody knows us; and the third of a bottle of Chianti couldn't intoxicate anybody!' I confess I prefer my own defence of my abandonment of teetotalism; but God bless the Canon, whose kindly temptation of that day was only one of a thousand things I owe to his affectionate care and guardianship. He sleeps amongst the people he loved, and the poor do not forget him. But he made it necessary for a logical person like myself to put my principles in order; and I decided to be in future what I called for want of a better title a territorial teetotaller. That is, I kept the pledge rigidly in Ireland, but took what was put before me elsewhere. (And that pledge I kept until 1923, when my mother, a woman of imperious character, ordered me to drink wine at her table; and I could not disobey my mother.) But the result of Canon O'Mahony's sophistry was that when Francis Meynell and I were being entertained at The Hague in the autumn of 1910 by the Chief Justice of the Supreme Court of Canada (and I believe that Sir Charles Fitzpatrick is still alive, although he must be of Nestorian age by now) I was enabled to drink at lunch the delicious Chablis of the Club of which he was an Honorary Member. After twenty-nine years I can still remember the clean glint of that wine, and my surprise at finding it so unsweet, for I thought of all wines in terms of sweetness in those days. I wish I could have noted the particulars of the growth; it was assuredly something excellent, probably a Vaudésir, or perhaps a 'La Moutonne', for those were the days before 'La Moutonne' had suffered eclipse. Whether it has yet been brought back to its pristine standard I am unable to say, for I have not drunk it for many years. But I had a correspondence with Monsieur Long Depaquit some years ago, in the course of which he assured me that he was doing all in his power to restore the ancient excellence of his wine. 'La Moutonne' was a little portion of his vineyard, not shown on the cadastral plan and therefore not subject to the Law of Place-names of Origin; in the old days the label meant that the wine was made from grapes grown on that particular favoured acre, but I could not get from the proprietor a clear statement whether the label was still so limited or whether he claimed the right to apply it to wine made from grapes grown elsewhere. For some time past the lists of Chablis published by writers on Burgundy have usually set Vaudésir at the head of the column, a place formerly occupied by 'La Moutonne'. My advice to those who drink such wines is, to judge them on their merits. Having mentioned these two vineyards, it is only fair to draw attention also to the excellence of 'Les Grenouilles', a wine of great delicacy.

For every bottle of genuine Chablis produced there are sold probably a hundred red bottles that are frauds. Browning is largely responsible. There are few students who have not chuckled over his monstrous rhyme:

Then I went indoors, brought out a loaf,
Half a cheese and a bottle of Chablis;
Lay on the grass and forgot the oaf
Over a jolly chapter of Rabelais.

Thence comes their familiarity with the name; 'What shall we drink?' 'Oh! why not a bottle of Chabelais?' '*Not* Chabelais; Chablis.' 'Have it your own way.' And, incidentally, I protest against accompanying bread and cheese with a bottle of Chablis. It should have been beer, even if that spoiled the rhyme; but if you *must* have bread and cheese with wine, you must drink something rough and coarse, like a cheap Côte Rotie or a very *ordinaire* Claret. Chablis, if good, deserves a more delicate background; and, if bad, is not worth drinking. And if he was lying on the grass, Browning was drinking his Chablis on a hot day, un-iced; a horrid thought. Chablis needs the attention of the ice-pail, as do nearly all white wines.

Without desiring to refine too much, I am not to be taken as suggesting that cheese and Chablis are hostile to one another; I merely say that Chablis is not the wine for a bread and cheese lunch. For a meal of that sort you want a good full cheese of the Cheddar kind, and the real cheese for Chablis is Gruyère. Even Brie and Camembert are too violent for it.

Maurice Healy *Stay Me With Flagons*, 1940, 1963

Mr Healy is right about Chablis. It's a lovely wine and with ever tightening restrictions on wine labelling you're much less likely now to get an inferior wine passed off as Chablis.

So as not to break the bank, again, try a Premier Cru, rather than the more expensive Grand Cru. I recommend Chablis Premier Cru Montmain.

The 1921 Yquem was a young wine then, and became a legend. I have drunk it twice since the day when it washed down my roast mutton in the Sauternais, but on both occasions in England and with fruit, so that it went down more comfortably.

What I remember best about it, though, is the story I was told by a girl I knew, early in the war, who had recently been divorced, and greatly to her surprise, by her much older and, hitherto, complaisant husband:

They had lived, she and the husband, in a stately Sussex home, the park of which had been turned by the War Office into a tented field, and its greater rooms into the officers' mess of a smart and rather rakish regiment. Its subalterns were not indifferent to the lady's charms – the lady herself not unduly prim, nor hard to please. It was somehow understood that neither the colonel nor the cuckolded husband would complain, so long as certain decencies or, to be more precise, certain reticences – were observed.

And yet . . . the blow fell. The lady and that evening's lover were discovered, when on other evenings with other young men her adventures had gone carefully unnoticed. She was turned out into the black-out at little more than a moment's notice, and divorced as quickly as a lady could.

It was long before she could understand why, she told me. Why that evening, and not on any other? And then it had dawned on her. Until that particular evening, she had dispensed her favours, by previous and prettily planned arrangement, in boudoir or in bedroom. It was an understood thing, and the eyes both of martial and of marital authority had winked at it. But on the particular, the fatal, evening she was showing off the house to a recently joined young officer, and they had reached the wine cellar which, in that house, was very properly a show-place. A look in his hostess's eye overwhelmed the boy; his ardour would not wait; and they were heard, and thus discovered, in such a position, she shyly intimated, as to be agitating the bin of Yquem 1921.

The husband was unduly hasty. Had he stopped to think, he would have remembered that white wines – even a twenty-year-old dessert wine – throw no deposit, or none to speak of, and shaking does them little harm. Now, had it been a bin of the 1920 Lafite (the great 1920 clarets were delicious drinking well into the 1960s) he would have been justified in having his wife dragged naked through the streets at the cart's tail, and slitting her lover's weazand . . .

Cyril and Elizabeth Ray *Wine With Food*, 1975

(We need a wine with 'good vibes, man' – that dates me.)

But this story is delightful. I can't though recommend Yquem again; that's against the rules. So I think a glass or two of Château Caillou from Barsac.

For above a week I lived within half an hour's walk of the most celebrated vineyards in Burgundy; and I cannot refrain from remarking that, however, agreeable the house of an Englishman may be, there is in that of a French gentleman a freedom from ceremony, an ease, and a charm that are not easily forgotten. If English travellers could pass some of their time in the domestic circles of French families, they would form an impression very different from that produced by coming in contact solely with those whose politeness is mercenary. Several of the vineyards belong to the gentleman I was visiting, and from him I learned the most minute details connected with them; but it would be tiresome and uninteresting to give here more than a general outline of their capabilities.

At Nuits, fifteen miles south of Dijon, are large cellars of wine, in which may be found all the kinds of the district. Vosne is a village two miles from Nuits, and close to it are Romanée-Conti, Romanée, La Tache, Grande Rue, Richebourg, and about a mile from those is Clos-Vougeôt, and a little farther off, nearer Dijon, is Chambertin. A goodly array of names! Except Clos-Vougeôt and Chambertin, not one of these yield on an average above 70 hogsheads, and Romanée-Conti seldom produces more than 12.

I could not remark any difference of flavour while eating the grapes, but I was assured that those accustomed to taste the wine, can immediately decide from which vineyard it has been made. The vines are old and of the best kinds: Romanée, Richebourg, La

Tache, and Grande Rue (the latter across the road), appear to have all an equally favourable aspect; but with all these apparent resemblances, there may be a stratum of soil which causes the difference perceptible to experienced local tasters. The palate, like the eye, the ear, or touch, acquires by practice various degrees of sensitiveness that would be incredible, were it not a well-ascertained fact. For instance, those who devote attention to it, can tell whether a salmon is Irish or Scotch, and others can distinguish those taken from different rivers. Anyone who has eaten a grouse from the southern parts of Scotland, can perceive how different the taste and flavour are from one of the Highlands, fed entirely upon the heather-berry.

These vineyards possess to the fullest extent the characteristics of the highest class of red burgundy, which are a brilliant deep colour, delicious aroma, full rich body, great softness and delicacy.

The Clos-Vougeôt is a large vineyard surrounded by a wall, and is so celebrated, that when a French regiment marches past, it halts and presents arms. It is much overrated, for, although the upper part on the acclivity produces wine, such as none other surpasses, still the declivity is not at all equal to it; and the lowest part is no better than many other vineyards in the neighbourhood. Such well cared-for vineyards will produce the best wines, even in the most unfavourable seasons; but like Château Lafitte of 1858, worth 70*l.* or 80*l.* and in 1860 only 5*l.* per hogshead, so Clos-Vougeôt may be worth 70*l.* or 80*l.* one year, and dear at 5*l.* in another season. The average produce of Clos-Vougeôt is about 500 hogsheads.

Another vineyard of justly high reputation is Chambertin, not far from Clos-Vougeôt; it yields generally about 150 hogsheads, which in a good year has a remarkably fine flavour. As those names are known throughout the world, it may well be imagined how rarely they can be obtained in a genuine state. But, besides these, there are many that should satisfy even very fastidious connoisseurs; and, for my part, I think some of them more agreeable than the celebrated growths, such as the La Tache or Richebourg, which are really too 'grand', and require many years' keeping in wood and in bottle before they are fit for use.

Thomas George Shaw *The Wine, the Vine, and the Cellar*, 1863

I spent some days in Burgundy this year, tasting from barrel and bottle, visiting the vineyards where the vines were just coming into flower. It was mid- to late-April, a fascinating time to view the vineyards as the demarcation lines between, say Bâtard-Montrachet and Bienvenues-Bâtard-Montrachet are still so clearly visible in the ground.

A hogshead, by the way, is a measure of volume for wine. However, there doesn't seem to be a clearly defined amount. The best I can say is that a hogshead is approximately 52½ Imperial gallons.

I think I have to go for a bottle of the either of the two aforementioned Montrachets. They are exquisite.

Warnings of gout on my own part, and the annoyance of finding more and more people leave such treasures in the decanter, prevented my buying much Burgundy latterly. My last batch was a comparatively humble Corton of 1881, bought when it was nineteen years old for sixty-eight shillings a dozen, and quite cheap at its price. It lasted for at least a dozen years longer, and never went off at all.

But in earlier days the Richebourg was accompanied by a bevy of less distinguished representatives of the Slope of Gold and its neighbourhood – Corton again, Pommard, Santenay, Chenas and others – beverage wines which you paid some forty shillings a dozen or less for, and could drink without reproach of conscience, even by yourself. The bin was the occasion of a pleasant occurrence, which I may tell to the glory of my family, and perhaps for the amusement of the reader. One of my father's sisters was a very old lady, who lived by herself in a remote part of the country on no large income, and (as the phrase goes) in a very quiet way. Having some trouble with her eyes, she came up to town to consult an oculist, and naturally stayed with me. The oculist, finding nothing organically wrong, but only a certain weakness of age and constitution, recommended her to drink Burgundy. I gave her on successive days some of the Richebourg, telling her frankly that it was a very expensive wine, and some of a sound Pommard, which could be had for between half and a third of the price, that she might choose and order some from the merchant, who, as it happened, supplied both. I had imagined that the first figure would either frighten or shock her; but she said with perfect simplicity, 'I think, my dear boy, the best always *is* the best,' and ordered a small supply of the Richebourg forthwith.

George Saintsbury *Notes on a Cellar-Book*, 1920

Richebourg is one of the truly great wines of the world and one of the most expensive, partly because of the tiny amount that is produced. Its average production between 1988 and 1992 was 2690 cases per year. Even that is quite a lot in comparison with La Romanée, considered by some the greatest of red Burgundies; sadly I've never tasted it. Its average production over the same period was 300 cases per year!

I can't go on suggesting you try these vastly expensive wines, so how about something from just down the road from Vosne-Romanée? Try some Morey-St-Denis AOC from Domaine Dujac.

I can only remember two lots of Burgundy in my own cellar that were outstanding . One was a magnificent Clos de Vougeôt 1904 that I got from Christopher's about 1925, the other was a Les Bonnes Mares 1921 that came from Avery's of Bristol. The latter was a less expensive wine, because it was younger and the vintage year was not classic; but it really proclaimed the true merit of Burgundy as loyally and satisfactorily as its elder superior in rank, which, however, was a superb wine: probably the best I ever had in my cellar. For let there be no doubt about it: Burgundy at its best overtops Claret at *its* best. You will only drink four or five bottles of truly first-class Burgundy in your whole life (and you will be lucky if you find so many; only three have rung that bell with me; good as the 1904 and the 1921 were, none of them was the really outstanding thing I have in mind), But you can drink Claret of the highest class several times in the year: Claret that should be drunk kneeling, with every sip consecrated as a libation to Heaven. I wonder if I can get an image from the orchestra. Everyone knows how tender and beautiful the flute can be in a solo part; but whosoever has had the luck to hear the solo played by the recorder recognizes a fullness, a roundness and a pathos of tone to which the flute cannot attain. Now Claret flutes for us all the time, while Burgundy is usually content to grate on its scrannel pipe of wretched straw. Occasionally it, too, will flute with grace and tenderness; but, once in a blue moon, it will produce the recorder, and then, indeed, our hearts are melted. Such a moment occurred to me the other day, when at the hospitable table of my good friend, Sir Francis Colchester-Wemyss, I partook of a bottle of Richebourg 1923 that fulfilled all the conditions that govern the best of Burgundy. I had honestly forgotten how good Burgundy could be, and this was like a new revelation.

Now, why should Burgundy be so uncertain and difficult when Claret is so easy and reliable? The answer is to be found in history. It is probable that the wines of Burgundy would never have burgeoned into so great a fame if it had not been for the fact that nearly all the great vineyards were founded by communities of monks, ensuring a continuous tradition of skilled attention to the wines and the vintage. In order that a wine may be relied on year after year, it is necessary that the whole vineyard should have the same care and that there should be continuity of practice. A vineyard belonging to Jean this year and to Jacques next year and to Paul the year after would not be likely to produce a wine of the same constancy as that produced under the continuous care of Robert. In the past, a community of monks always proved the most satisfactory nurserymen; there was no sudden change of ownership brought about by death or alienation, and the tradition of the vineyard passed from hand to hand almost imperceptibly. Under such care the great vineyards of Burgundy achieved their excellence; around them were grouped smaller estates, whose owners were not above learning from the monks, and who gradually spread the art of wine-making far and wide throughout the district.

Maurice Healy *Stay Me With Flagons*, 1940, 1963

Here Mr Healy has come up with something of great interest.

According to my research, the monks laid out the vineyards in the eleventh century and many remain exactly the same to this day.

The wine selected has to be Clos de Vougeôt – the 1985 is excellent.

Cave de Sologny, Pinot de Bourgogne '76

The south of Burgundy rising to the occasion. Vigorous ripe Pinot Noir is always attractive young, but this really wants twelve months in the bottle for the birdsong of last summer to come through properly.

Hugh Johnson *Sunday Times* (quoted in *Private Eye*, 'Pseuds Corner')

Avoiding appearing in Pseuds Corner can be difficult for the wine writer, even the great Hugh Johnson. If he'd used the words 'scents' instead of 'birdsong' he'd have probably got away with it. You have to choose between lyrical romanticism (Johnson) or the pithily mundane (Jilly Goolden) – 'It has a bouquet like freshly sharpened pencils'.

I can enjoy both and Cave de Sologny, Pinot de Bourgogne would certainly be worth listening to.

In short, it was weather which rendered inconceivable such things as illness, bad harvests, earthquakes, the end of the world, or any other catastrophe; weather to make you sleep soundly, recover your taste for your wife, stop boxing the children's ears, forget to count your money, and merely watch the happy flow of events in a world where optimism knows no bounds.

It was this which to some extent was Clochemerle's undoing. While Nature was doing all the work, swelling the grapes with alcohol, the people, with but little to occupy them, fell into a debauchery of speech, poking their noses into other people's business, interfering with each other's love affairs. At the same time they drank rather more than they should on account of that confounded heat which drew all the moisture out of your body and brought you constant trickles of perspiration. Each of these was dried by a little breeze, which came in puffs and crept into armpits, shoulder blades, hollows between breasts, and curves of buttocks, and beneath skirts of loose pattern, cut wide to give ease and freedom to all they concealed – which itself was ready enough for frolic. In short, it was absolutely and entirely the most amazingly fine splendid weather that you could possibly imagine!

Alas, we mortals here below are strangely made, fashioned all awry, it may well be said; wretched addlepated creatures who might as well go hang ourselves. When we have all we want to make us happy – sunshine, good wine, fine women, a surfeit of them, and long days for the enjoyment of all this – we must needs go and spoil everything ultimately derived. The vocabulary of Clochemerle, forcible and vivid, has a racy flavor of its own.

What the Clochemerle fête was like, with such summer weather as this, may readily be imagined. Beginning on the morning of August 15th, there were feasting and carousal, with vast quantities of chickens which had been trussed the day before, rabbits kept in pickle for forty-eight hours, hares which had been poached in snares, tarts kneaded at home and baked in the oven at the baker's, crayfish, snails, hot sausages – indeed so many good things that the women in the houses took turns at the kitchen range. The sole topic of conversation between neighbors was food.

On the evening of the 15th, stomachs were already distended, having had more than their customary fill. The best dishes had nevertheless been reserved for the following day, for the inhabitants of Clochemerle are not people to boggle at the idea of two consecutive days of feasting. As soon as night fell, there were illuminations and a torchlight tattoo. Then a dance was set in train in the main square, where a platform for the musicians and the 'wine fountain' had been made ready.

This wine fountain is a Clochemerle custom. Under the direction of the town council, casks are set up and tapped, and everyone is free to drink to his heart's content as long as the fête lasts. Volunteers are found for the purpose of replenishing the casks – which are encased in straw to keep the wine fresh – at frequent intervals.   At the side of the fountain large slates are placed, on which are inscribed by a special jury the names of men who wish to compete for the title of 'Champion Drinker', which is conferred every year on the individual who has imbibed the most.   This jury exercises the utmost care in marking up the points, for the title is one which is keenly sought after.   The most famous Champion Drinker that Clochemerle has ever known was a man called Pistachet, who once drank in four days three hundred and twenty glasses of wine.   This exploit goes back to the year 1887, and expert opinion holds that this record will stand for all time. Moreover, at the time he made it, Pistachet was at the zenith of his powers (he was thirty), and though he retained his title for another ten years, from that time onwards his capacity was steadily on the wane.   He died at the age of forty-four from cirrhosis of the liver, which had reached such a point that that organ had degenerated into a mere abscess and burst in his body.   But his name will live forever.

In 1923 the title of Champion Drinker had been held for three years by the postman Blazot.   He was in excellent training and as the time for keeping up his reputation approached, he was regularly drinking his sixty glasses a day.   But he himself was well on the road to cirrhosis and was showing signs of weakness.   To wrest the title from him was François Toumignon's secret ambition.

Gabriel Chevallier *Clochemerle,* 1936 trans. Jocelyn Godefroi, 1985

Sixty glasses a day – that's twelve bottles!   I know this is fiction, but the thought of such consumption gives me a hangover as I read.

Hangover cures are something we haven't touched on. There really is only one and that is sleep aided by copious amounts of water.   If, however, you can't sleep until midday the next morning, then toy with a soft-boiled egg and soldiers at about 1.30 followed by paracetamol, not aspirin.

I find that a hearty fried breakfast works wonders.   I know this sounds crazy, but it works for me.   I suppose it may be something to do with my liver, straining away to process the alcohol from the night before, suddenly being confronted by another intruder, large quantities of fat. This so shocks the liver that it turns its full attention to breakfast and pushes the hangover into the background. This theory has no basis in medical science and on rereading what I've written, I begin to fear for my sanity.

I can only drink large quantities (over a bottle) of the lightest of white wines, but I'm sure the wine fountain in Clochemerle was running with red wine, so for me a light red, or rosé. Now there's a good idea. Try a Rosé de Loire AOC from Domaine de Varinelles.

In Poperinghe in 1916 the best-known of the war restaurants was in the Square; it was called 'La Poupée', and a mother and her unlimited family of daughters served meals of which the best Paris houses need not have been ashamed. The youngest girl cannot have been more than ten years old, but she joked with the officers with a readiness of repartee that would have done credit to a young lady of twice her age. Some years ago I saw a letter in *The Times* stating that this war-baby was getting married, and asking that those who still remembered 'Ginger' would contribute to a wedding present. I believe that the result was enormous. I hope that poor Ginger is not caught up in the present war as well.

But it was not about Ginger that I meant to write, but about the wine we drank at 'La Poupée'. Remember, I was to all intents and purposes a teetotaller in those days; but I had learned in the trenches how a glass of Port could restore a chilled circulation, and I was not averse to try a few experiments in pleasanter surroundings. So at the dinners that we used to take when out of the line we used to bid Madame to bring us a bottle of 'Courage'. And she would place upon the table a bottle of the Burgundy shape, bearing the label 'Moulin-à-Vent, 1911'. You will observe that the wine was five years old, which is a good age at which to drink Beaujolais. They mature their wine in casks rather longer than in Burgundy proper or Bordeaux, sometimes not bottling until five years after the vintage. This particular wine must have been a good while in bottle, for it had grown to like its new home, and was entirely free from the vices of new-bottled wine. It had a beautiful colour, not so light as to suggest very late bottling, but at the same time lighter than the usual Claret or Burgundy. It had a very full bouquet, rather of the raspberry variety. It was a balanced wine; it appealed to every sense, and you could drink a couple of bottles of it without being aware that it was having any effect upon you; I will not answer for what the neighbours thought. But to that Moulin-à-Vent 1911 I owe my most grateful thanks; not only because of the comfort that it then gave me, but because it was that wine that taught me to like the taste and bouquet of red wine. Claret followed, but much later. I did not then know, nor indeed do I know with certainty now, but I believe that Moulin-à-Vent is the name of a district in Romanèche-Thorins, and there are several separate vineyards that are entitled to use the name, each of them having a distinguishing label of its own which I have never seen, nor do I know any of their names. Here one must trust that one's wine-merchant has bought from a reliable Beaujolais shipper; I venture to guess that the separate vineyards are each on the small side, and that they submit to blending, like the small Burgundians.

Maurice Healy *Stay Me With Flagons*, 1940, 1963

Here is a charming reminiscence which has just beneath the surface hints of the absolute horror of the First World War; calling the wine 'Courage' and recalling the 'comfort it gave me'. I don't think any of my generation can fully comprehend the bravery of millions of men and women in both world wars, but to leave the lice- and rat-infested trenches to sit and eat and drink good food and wine must have been like moving from hell to heaven. Indeed, had I been there I think I would have found the contrast unbearable.

A bottle of Moulin-à-Vent – it *can* be very good.

What is the nastiest dish or drink you can possibly invent or imagine?

The poser was set as a daft, after-dinner competition one ribald evening, and the easy winner – streets ahead of concoctions so imaginatively vile that they could not be written even on a lavatory wall – was the simplest: a soup-plate of warm gin with a red hair in it.

When I recounted this to Nick Clarke, the larger-than-life character who runs Nick's Diner in darkest Fulham, he said that he had beaten a fellow-restaurateur in a similar contest with his creation: tram-driver's glove *en croûte*, in Brylcreem sauce.

I can think of nothing so nasty as either of these, but I still remember the British tycoon I met on holiday at a French hotel, who drank Mouton-Rothschild 1953 at every lunch and dinner ('very reliable people, the Rothschilds, o'boy'), washing it down each time with a tin of coca-Cola, because red wine makes you so thirsty, o'boy.

And Wynford Vaughan-Thomas tells the story of the *vin d'honneur* given by the HQ staff of General Patch's United States Seventh army during the liberation of Burgundy to General de Montsabert and other distinguished French comrades-in-arms.

It was held, Wynford recounts, in an eighteenth-century palace in Besançon: 'trumpets sounded, and a column of waiters marched in, bearing bottles on silver trays. My heart gave a warning thump – the bottles were from Burgundy, the noblest gifts of the Côte and, horror of horrors, they were bubbling gently . . .'

'We're in luck,' whispered a United States colonel in Wynford's ear. 'The doc knows all about this Frog liquor: he's hotted it up with surgical spirit . . .'

Cyril and Elizabeth Ray *Wine With Food*, 1975

Horror of Horrors! But fine wines can be ruined by far less cavalier treatment as most wine buffs know to their regret.

It seems an insult to nominate a wine, let alone a French wine, in these circumstances. Let them drink Coke.

PATTISONS' WHISKY

FORGING AHEAD

Pattisons' Whisky, like a British Ironclad, is at home in all "Waters."

ASK FOR { 'PATTISONS' and Schweppe. / 'PATTISONS' and Soda. } 'PATTISONS' and Apollinaris. / 'PATTISONS' and St. Ronans.

At first acquaintance you will not care much for *pic-à-pou* or the wine of the country [the French Pyrenees], but with patience you may possibly learn to appreciate the Vin de Jurançon. Tradition has it that Henri Quatre's nurses preferred to give this form of nourishment rather than the Mellin's Food of the time. Perhaps babies were differently constituted in those days.

In any case you will always be able to get a good bottle of claret, bearing the name of some first-class Bordeaux firm, such as Johnson, Barton Guestier, or Luze, etc. If you are lucky enough to obtain a glass of genuine old Armagnac, you will probably rank it, as a liqueur, very nearly as high as any cognac you have ever tasted.

A word of warning! Don't be too eager to order whisky and soda. The 'Scotch' is not of uniform quality.

Lt-Col Nathaniel Newnham-Davis and Algernon Bastard *The Gourmet's Guide to Europe*, 1903

I bet the Scotch wasn't of 'uniform quality'. Sometimes in life you do things that are just asking for trouble.

A bottle of Jurançon AOC – this isn't easy to get hold of outside South-West France. It's a white wine and at its best is slightly sweet and spicy.

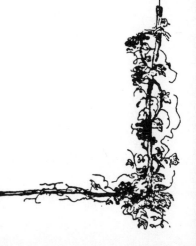

Algernon: Why is it that at a bachelor's establishment the servants invariably drink the champagne? I ask merely for information.

Lane: I attribute it to the superior quality of the wine, sir. I have often observed that in married households the champagne is rarely of a first-rate brand.

Oscar Wilde *The Importance of Being Earnest*, 1895

I went to a school called Bedales, whose founder, J H Badeley, was a very spry nonagenarian when I was there in the sixties. As a young man he had known Oscar Wilde and used to tell this story.

Wilde was a weekend guest at a house party in the home counties. From Friday afternoon to Monday morning he dazzled his fellow guests with his wit. The whole party was in his thrall and six or seven of them went to see him off at the station on the Monday morning. With immaculate timing Wilde delivered his final *bon mot,* closed his carriage window, sat down and opened his newspaper just as the train moved off. However, it only moved a few feet before coming to a halt. The house guests, eager for an encore, moved up the platform and stood in an expectant group outside Wilde's carriage. There he sat behind his newspaper and never uttered a word for the full ten minutes it took for the train to start moving again. The performance was over.

I have to recommend champagne to go with Wilde, anything else seems inappropriate. Try a good demi-sec. It's not easy to get hold if but it's worth the effort. Don't think that it's going to be sweet; a good one is exactly as its name implies, half-dry. My favourite is made by Michel Arnould.

A man who sets you down to a driblet of champagne – who gives you a couple of beggarly glasses between the courses, and winks to John who froths up the liquor in your glass, and screws up the remainder of the bottle for his master's next day's drinking – such a man is an impostor and despicable snob . . . If money is an object to you, drink water . . . but if there is to be champagne, have no stint of it, in the name of Bacchus . . . When people have had plenty of champagne, they fancy they have been treated liberally. If you wish to save, save upon your hocks, sauternes, and moselles, which count for nothing, but disappear down careless throats like so much toast and water.

William Makepeace Thackeray (1811-63) *Miscellaneous Papers*

The village of Mougins in the South of France has more good restaurants than any village is really entitled to. One of the best is the Relais à Mougins; the owner/chef is Monsieur Surmain. On my first visit I ordered a bottle of champagne as an aperitif. The bottle was brought to the table, opened and tasted and then decanted into a rather beautiful, silver-topped claret jug. At the end of the meal, which was superb, Monsieur Surmain did his rounds of the tables and I asked him in my awful, halting French why he decanted his champagne. He replied that the first chef he worked for decanted his champagne because 'it is such a beautiful wine it seems a pity to hide it in a green bottle' and Surmain thought that one day, when he had his own restaurant, he would do the same. His reply, by the way, was delivered in faultless and accentless English: Monsieur Surmain had spent most of the war living in Whitstable Bay with an English nanny.

I find unexpected bilinguality unnerving. The Englishman in a country whose language he doesn't speak, or even worse attempts to speak, knowing in his heart that most of what he utters is ungrammatical baby talk, is not the most secure of travellers. And to be suddenly confronted by someone whose mastery of his native tongue is as good as his own produces a wave of almost disabling inadequacy, coupled with a primeval envy of such a gift.

As an alternative to champagne there are some wonderful sparkling wines. Try some Blanc de Blancs brut from Philippe Hérard.

To produce a hogshead of wine [champagne], it is calculated that from 769 to 960 pounds of grapes are required, according to the quantity of juice from the three first *pressings.* In Verzenay, Bouzy, Ambonnay, and other parts of the Montagne, the sales are by *caques* (tubs), of which there are from 5½ to 6½ to a hogshead of wine. The temptation to increase the quantity at the expense of the quality has been as powerful here as elsewhere; and not a few vineyards, once celebrated for their excellence, have fallen into such disrepute that many houses will not allow a grape from them to enter their cellar. There is a large extent of ground covered with vines, yielding the very choicest, and also a fine second class. The champagne sold at very low prices is from the low-lying grounds in the neighbouring districts, and from the bad vintages which are rejected by houses who desire to uphold the character of their brands.

The wine is next drawn off the lees into fresh casks, placed in stores above ground, where it remains till the month of March, when the important operation of bottling begins. This is a peculiarly anxious affair, for two results are desired: first, that the wine shall sparkle; and next, that its effervescence shall not be so forcible as to break too many bottles. As a guide and protection, a Gleucœnomêtre is used, to show the quantity of natural sugar, an overabundance of which causes great breakage. If it is found, for instance, that there are 9 degrees, there will be added 4 or 5 degrees of dissolved sugar-candy, so as to bring it up to 13 or 14 degrees, which is the quantity of saccharine usually required to produce a beautiful sparkling (*mousse*). Some firms have a constant stock of stout old wines in wood, nearly still, which is used to diminish the effervescence of the young kinds, by the addition of more or less at the time of bottling.

By this means, the appearance of age is given; and wine which, without this process, would be unfit for travelling, is often sent off when not a year old. The violence of the fermentation being thus subdued, the carbonic acid gas becomes less powerful, and the amount of breakage is diminished. Some bottles are much better and stronger than others, and no consideration of price should deter the purchase of the very best glass, as the one or the other may make a difference of 20 per cent. in the breakage. The use of the Saccharometer, the skilful blendings of different growths, and greater experience, have all tended to diminish this serious item in the cost of champagne. In former years, it was frequently enormous, especially in very hot seasons. I have known it as much as 60 and 70 per cent. In such years, when the grape is rich in saccharine, peculiar care is directed to place the young wines in the deepest and coldest vaults, and ice is frequently placed in them. In some cellars there are large ice-houses. The average breakage is now from 6 to 10 per cent.

If it is wished that the effervescence should come quickly, the bottles are kept in store above ground, and binned there; but if this is not desired, they are lowered into the cold deep cellars, binned in masses of thousands of bottles, in a most ingenious way, in the centre of the vault, the whole supported by a few laths; and although perfectly safe, the bin may be moved by pushing with the hand. An English cellarman laughs when told of it, and will not believe in its safety.

But even in the cold cellar, with the thermometer at 36° of Fahrenheit, the wine is not long in beginning to 'work', which shows itself by a slight bubbling in the bottles, reports as of pistols in all directions, and glass flying about, so that at this period wire-gauze protectors over the face are worn, when passing the bins. I know one cellar in which there are three men, who have each lost an eye owing to this cause. Along each bin a narrow gutter is cut, through which the lost liquid flows.

Notwithstanding the depth and the cold of the cellar, the changes in the external atmosphere produce a very decided effect; and the breakage is always greater in the spring, when the grape is budding, and in the autumn, when it is ripening, than at any other period of the year. The same is observed with other kinds in our docks, and it is attributed to the sympathy of the produce of the grape with the plant of its origin; but it would probably be more correct to trace it to the moisture and the atmospheric changes which usually then prevail. Some bottles break so entirely that all the contents pass to the floor and gutter; others retain a portion of the wine, which would soon become acid, if not removed; and, if this is not practicable, buckets of very cold water are thrown over them, to wash away any wine remaining in the broken bottles. Were this not carefully attended to, and the conduits and the floor

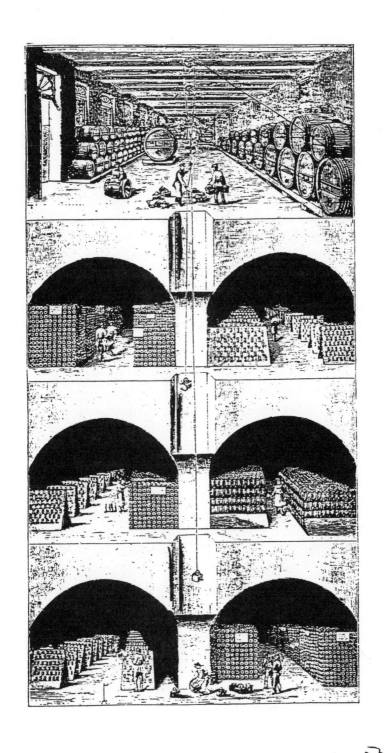

kept clear of wine, fermentation would arise, and the cellar would become impregnated with carbonic acid gas and putridity. The wine of the previous vintage being bottled in March, if it has been well made, will have attained its full effervescence by the end of October; when each bottle of the cuvée is examined, to see whether there are any on ullage – that is, that have leaked; these are filled up from other bottles.

The whole are then removed to another cellar, where they are re-binned; but, before doing this, each bottle is turned upside down, and shaken, so as to remove the deposit which has fallen, to the lowest interior side. They now remain untouched, except by their own occasional breakages, till a merchant of Reims, Epernay, &c., purchases them for preparation in his own way. They are then sent in their 'brût' (raw) state; and it would somewhat astonish those accustomed to the limpid fluid, to see it and to taste it before it has undergone the process of disgorging and sugar-candying. If its destination is out of the district or abroad, it must undergo much manipulation.

Whatever quantity is wanted, is taken from the large bin, every bottle is well shaken, in order to distribute the sediment through the bottle, which is then placed on a table full of holes, cut in such a way that it lies, mouth downwards, at an angle of 45°. This is called placing on point. In a few days, the deposit will be found on the lower shoulder. A peculiar sharp movement with the hand is given, to cause the deposit to get nearer the bottom of the cork; and this is done daily to every bottle for about three weeks, gradually bringing them all nearer the perpendicular. On examination, it will be found that the wine in the bottle is perfectly brilliant, and that the whole of the deposit has been brought to the bottom of the cork. To get rid of this with as little loss as possible and the prevention of any falling back into the wine, requires skill, experience and a steady hand. The operation is called disgorging – that is, taking from the neck.

The *dégorgeur* (disgorger), lifts the bottle very carefully, head slanting down, and cuts the string which holds the cork; this immediately flies, the wine rushes out, but at the same moment he jerks the bottle up and turns the mouth once or twice round, so as to let a little flow and carry off any bits of cork, &c., that might

otherwise fall back into the bottle. He pushes a cork in, and his part is finished, probably with the loss of less than a glass.

The bottle is now taken by the *vidangeur* (familiarly called *chopineur*), who pours out a certain quantity, according to the percentage of saccharine which he has been told is to be added. The third sharer in the labour, called the *opéreur,* now comes into play. He has before him, usually in a tin vessel, liquid sugar-candy, of which he puts into each bottle the quantity ordered, by means of a small measure, of which there are several sizes. In all respectable champagne houses this is the only 'adulteration' which the wine undergoes, and, were it not for the liqueur, few – those not excepted who talk about liking it very *dry* – would care to drink champagne.

It may be overdone as well as underdone; and, as in most things the difficulty is to attain the *juste-milieu,* no rule can be laid down; for some qualities require more than others; and this is the case when one year has well ripened the grapes, and another has left them green and harsh. Generally about 12 or 13 per cent. is enough, but some houses add even 15, 16, or more. Supposing the *vin brut* to be the same, the distinguishing character belonging to certain houses arises almost entirely from their liqueur, and how they apply it. Some have it perfectly pure and white, with a very slight addition of brandy or colour; others add a good deal of brandy, and also of colour, giving the appearance of body and the various shades of 'amber', 'partridge-eye', &c.; others consider that their liqueur is improved by being boiled.

Liqueurs, however prepared, but especially with colour and spirit, are very much improved by being kept for many years, as is frequently done, to render them soft and mellow, and less likely to deposit in bottle. Let anyone, however, who can appreciate and distinguish pure from brandied and coloured champagne, compare one with liqueur neither brandied nor coloured, against the other; and he will immediately perceive in the former a fine delicate bouquet with purity of taste, while there is in the other coarseness both of taste and flavour, and a frequent want of brilliancy, if long in bottle.

Till lately, champagne was considered thin and poor, unless altered from its natural state; and the only kind in vogue was such as no man in Champagne, and few anywhere else, except in England, would drink. For liqueuring, there has lately been a beautiful little machine invented, by which each bottle receives a certain quantity only. It possesses the further advantage of a very slight escape of gas in comparison with the process by hand.

The bottle now passes to the *récouleur,* whose duty it is to fill up to the proper height. It then comes to the fifth, the *boucheur,* or corker. The sixth, the *ficeleur,* or stringer, fastens down the cork by string. The seventh, the *ficeleur au fil de fer,* performs a similar operation with wire. The eighth, usually a woman, places the silver or gold foil over the cork and neck; and the ninth wraps the bottle in paper, when it is ready for packing.

Thomas George Shaw *The Wine, the Vine and the Cellar,* 1863

This is an informative guide to the making of champagne. Although written years ago, the basic principles, as far as I know, haven't changed. The image of an unfortunate cellarman staggering into daylight covered in blood from champagne shrapnel is a little alarming, but I think to be maimed by an exploding bottle of Krug has a certain cachet, whereas a painful accident that befell an acquaintance of mine has none at all.

He had returned home very drunk and was just climbing into bed when the idea that he must brush his teeth sprang to the forefront of his mind. He slid out of bed and swayed down the darkened corridor to the nearby bathroom where indeed he gave his teeth a vigorous scrubbing. He then started his return journey bearing back to bed with him, for reasons more to do with Latour than logic, his toothbrush. The result was that when he tripped over his cat he stabbed himself severely injuring, though fortunately not blinding, his right eye.

Another alternative to champagne, and this one may surprise you, is Asti Spumante. At its best it is wonderful, especially with puddings. Try to get hold of a bottle by Giulio Cocchi.

Venice, 21 August. After inspecting two palaces, the Labiena, containing Tiepolo's fresco of Cleopatra's Banquet, and the Pappadopoli, a stifling labyrinth of plush and royal photographs, we took sanctuary from culture in Harry's Bar. There was an ominous chatter, a quick-fire of greetings: the English are arriving.

In the evening we went back to Harry's Bar, where our host regaled us with a drink compounded of champagne and cherry brandy. 'To have the right effect,' said Harry confidentially, 'it must be the worst cherry brandy.' It was.

Before this my acquaintance with our host was limited to the hunting field. He looked unfamiliar in a green beach vest and white mess jacket.

Robert Byron The Road to Oxiana, 1937

Harry's Bar in Venice is still renowned and rightly so, but the only drink to have there as far as I'm concerned is a Bellini. This combines the juice and pulp of fresh, blood-red peaches and champagne. Vigorously mixed and served foaming and pink in a large glass, as an aperitif it has few rivals.

As to the champagnes found abroad, unless they are specially made for the English market, they must not be judged from an English standpoint, being as a rule far too sweet for our taste.

An instance of this occurred to me at Rheims, when staying with one of the champagne magnates for some shooting owned by a syndicate of some of the large champagne shippers. We met for *déjeuner* at their Châlet de Chasse or club-house, each gentleman bringing his own wine. The result was that one saw from ten to a dozen different famous brands of champagne on the table.

My host asked me which sort I would prefer. 'Du vin Brut, if you have any,' I replied. 'Ah! Vous buvez de ce poison-là?' exclaimed he, smiling. So they evidently did not agree with our taste for dry wine. But you can make a pleasant and harmless drink of the sweet champagne in summer by mixing it with an equal quantity of light Moselle, adding a liqueur glass of curaçao, and putting some wild strawberries or a large peach cut up into the concoction with some ice.

Lt-Col Nathaniel Newnham-Davis and Algernon Bastard *The Gourmet's Guide to Europe*, 1903

Sweet champagne is denoted by the word 'Rich' on the neck label. I've only drunk it once or twice and most successfully when poured over a bowl of summer fruits.

In the days of the Consul Plancus the City of Cork was a haven for all sorts of unexpected argosies, some of the most agreeable being theatrical and musical. Indeed, the late Sir Frank Benson saw to it that the young idea in Cork should be enabled to shoot along the most approved lines; his annual visits gave us three weeks of delightful education, and he was pleased to say to me half a dozen years ago that he had found the Cork audiences amongst the most critically appreciative he had ever faced. The Compton Comedy

Company was another regular visitor; while to the musical stage came Arthur Rouseby, Carl Rosa and Charles Manners with their respective companies; and we were enabled to hear some of the most distinguished vocalists of the day. Nor were these our only loves. There was a sincere but unpretentious body called the Elster-Grime Opera Company that used to take the lesser stage of the Palace Theatre and give rattling good performances of the lighter Verdi and similar operas; after forty years I have a vivid recollection of a presentation of *The Daughter of the Regiment* that nothing at the Opéra Comique in Paris could banish from my memory. And suddenly we learned of a still more gallant effort; the G. Hilton St. Just Grand Opera Company had engaged the Assembly Rooms for three weeks, with G. Hilton St. Just himself singing all the tenor parts. The city buzzed with the excitement of pleasurable anticipation. We heard with delight that our excellent Lord Mayor, Mr. Augustine Roche, himself a keen patron of music and the arts, intended to give them a civic welcome; and, as Mr. Roche in private life was a wine merchant, we had no doubt that the company would be well entertained. Nor were our ideas erroneous. The reception took place at 6 p.m., and the performance of *La Traviata* began at 8 p.m. I had secured a good seat, and while waiting for the overture to begin I could hear that the Lord Mayor's hospitality had been transferred to the stage; the popping of corks was intermittent but frequent. But punctually at eight the orchestra appeared; it consisted of a pianist and a harmonium player; I think that sometimes a flautist joined them, when not engaged in singing on the stage. But courage conquers all; a creditable performance of the overture took place, and the curtain rose upon the revel of the first act. The cast were dressed in eighteenth-century costumes; but Mr. Roche's waiters lent a modern note, and continued to uncork Champagne with an assiduity and a hospitality that filled me with direful presages. Never was the drinking song rendered with greater gusto; the chorus splashed Champagne in every direction, and the principals sang with the chorus. Mr. G. Hilton St. Just, no mean tenor, was in excellent voice; and I felt that for once, if I was not getting exactly what Verdi had intended, I was undoubtedly enjoying the authentic atmosphere which Dumas had meant to create. But

Nemesis was at hand. The volatile wine carried the company through the first act with tremendous *élan;* but when the curtain rose for the second it soon became evident that there was something rotten in the state of Denmark. When Alfredo's father came to reason with his son, the latter sat down at a table and buried his face in his hands; at the end of each line of the Di Provenza he lifted it, glared at his father, and buried it again; occasionally a sob of emotion (which looked uncommonly like a hiccup) shook his body. Meantime his father, who enjoyed a powerful bass-baritone, kept alternating between hissed pianissimi and thundered fortissimi, something like this:

> Far aWAY *in old Provence we have* WAI*ted thy return;*
> *We have waited* THY RETURN *far away in old Provence.*

By this time there was no restraining the gallery. ' 'Gor, boys! 'Tis great stuff Gussie's been givin' 'em!' cried one voice, and fifty others joined in a chorus of not unfriendly chaff, which did not affect the performers in the slightest. The opera finished triumphantly, Mr. St. Just's final 'O Violetta!' being a magnificent degeneration from a musical note into a hysterical sobbing. Never had Champagne a more agreeable triumph. And if I know my Gussie Roche, it was no mere non-vintage wine that was being offered; it was probably the 1900 vintage and a first-class brand.

I have told that story because I think it illustrates several of the qualities of Champagne. In the first place there is no wine which will work more quickly as a pick-me-up or a banisher of constraint. It is amusing to observe the frozen silence which usually attends the opening of a dinner-party, and which vanishes in a buzz of conversation as soon as the Champagne has been round. The late Horatio Bottomley had many demerits; but he was clever enough to appreciate the value of a good draught of Champagne at eleven o'clock in the morning. Harry Preston used to say that eleven o'clock was the ideal hour for the wine; just a chicken sandwich and a pint. For many years it was my habit to begin my celebration of Christmas by attending midnight Mass, and then partaking of a very early morning breakfast consisting of some of the delicious spiced beef of which Messieurs Russell of Cork appear to have the monopoly, home-made brown bread and butter and a bottle of Champagne. My subsequent sleep was peaceful, and I awoke, filled with Christian charity towards all men – or almost all. The very appearance of a bottle of Champagne on the table gives an uplift to the spirits; and anything that does that in evil days deserves a decoration, well represented by the gold-foil around the neck of the bottle.

Maurice Healy *Stay Me With Flagons*, 1940, 1963

I wonder when the last civic reception was given to an artist from a pop group to sculptor, by an English city council?

Another mixed champagne aperitif – buy a bottle of Crême de Pêche de Vigne made by Jean Philippe Marchand in Gevrey-Chambertin. It's not cheap, about £14 a bottle, but it will last a long time. This liqueur is made from the small red peaches that grow in his vineyards. You could call the drink the Cheat's Bellini. Put a small amount in the bottom of a glass and fill it with champagne. When you open the Crême de Pêche do take a sniff at the bottle, the smell is uplifting!

I *can* drink, and bear a good deal of wine (as you may recollect in England): but it don't exhilarate – it makes me savage and suspicious. Laudanum has a similar effect; but I can take much of it without any effect at all. The thing that gives me the highest spirits (it seems absurd, but true) is a dose of *salts* – I mean in the afternoon, after their effect. But one can't take *them* like champagne.

George Gordon, Lord Byron – Letter to Thomas Moore, 1830

So, Byron drank Andrew's Liver Salts from his skull drinking cup, answering my earlier query, if it does rather dent the Byronic image.

One of the greatest champagnes I have ever tasted was a magnum of thirty-year-old Krug from the Krug collection. If you win the lottery . . .

Wines from Valtellina, the district of northern Lombardy almost on the border between Italy and Switzerland, became particular favourites of the nineteenth-century traveller, John Addington Symonds. He spent several years living in Switzerland where he became something of a connoisseur of the dry, red wines which in those days had to be drawn by horses over high Alpine passes to fledgeling Swiss resorts like Davos and Klosters. Here he describes a journey by horse-drawn sleigh along the wine route from Davos across the mountains in the winter of 1881-82.

Valtelline wines bought in the wood vary, of course, according to their age and year of vintage. I have found that from 2.50 fr. to 3.50 fr. per litre is a fair price for sorts fit to bottle. The new wine of 1881 sold in the following winter at prices varying from 1.05 fr. to 1.80 fr. per litre.

It is customary for the Graubünden wine-merchants to buy up the whole produce of a vineyard from the peasants at the end of the vintage. They go in person or depute their agents to inspect the wine, make their bargains, and seal the cellars where the wine is stored. Then, when the snow has fallen, their own horses with sleighs and trusted servants go across the passes to bring it home. Generally they have some local man of confidence at Tirano, the starting-point for the homeward journey, who takes the casks up to that place and sees them duly charged. Merchants of old standing maintain relations with the same peasants, taking their wine regularly; so that from Lorenz Gredig at Pontresina or Andreas Gredig at Davos Dörfli, from Fanconi at Samaden, or from Giacomi at Chiavenna, special qualities of wine, the produce of certain vineyards, are to be obtained. Up to the present time this wine trade has been conducted with simplicity and honesty by both the dealers and the growers. One chief merit of Valtelline wine is that it is pure. How long so desirable a state of things will survive the slow but steady development of an export business may be questioned.

With so much practical and theoretical interest in the produce of the Valtelline to stimulate my curiosity, I determined to visit the district at the season when the wine was leaving it. It was the winter of 1881-82, a winter of unparalleled beauty in the high Alps. Day succeeded day without a cloud. Night followed night with steady stars, gliding across clear mountain ranges and forests of dark pines unstirred by wind. I could not hope for a more prosperous season; and indeed I made such use of it, that between the months of January and March I crossed six passes of the Alps in open sleighs – the Fluela, Bernina, Splügen, Julier, Maloja, and Albula – with less difficulty and discomfort in mid-winter than the traveller may often find on them in June.

At the end of January, my friend Christian and I left Davos long before the sun was up, and ascended for four hours through the interminable snow-drifts of the Fluela in a cold grey shadow. The sun's light seemed to elude us. It ran along the ravine through which we toiled; dipped down to touch the topmost pines above our heads; rested in golden calm upon the Schiahorn at our back; capriciously played here and there across the Weisshorn on our left, and made the precipices of the Schwartzhorn glitter on our right. But athwart our path it never fell until we reached the very summit of the pass. Then we passed quietly into the full glory of the winter morning – a tranquil flood of sunbeams, pouring through air of crystalline purity, frozen and motionless. White peaks and dark brown rocks soared up, cutting a sky of almost purple blueness. A stillness that might be felt brooded over the whole world; but in that stillness there was nothing sad, no suggestion of suspended vitality. It was the stillness rather of untroubled health, of strength omnipotent but unexerted . . .

All that upland wilderness is lovelier now than in the summer; and on the morning of which I write, the air itself was far more summery than I have ever known it in the Engadine in August. We could scarcely bear to place our hands upon the woodwork of the sleigh because of the fierce sun's heat. And yet the atmosphere was crystalline with windless frost. As though to increase the strangeness of these contrasts, the pavement of beaten snow was stained with red drops spilt from wine-casks which pass over it . . .

When we came to the galleries which defend the road from avalanches, we saw ahead of us a train of over forty sledges ascending, all charged with Valtelline wine. Our postilions drew up at the inner side of the gallery, between massive columns of the purest ice dependent from the rough-hewn roof and walls of rock.

A sort of open *loggia* on the farther side framed vignettes of the Valtelline mountains in their hard cerulean shadows and keen sunlight. Between us and the view defiled the wine-sledges; and as each went by, the men made us drink out of their *trinketti*. These are oblong, hexagonal wooden kegs, holding about fourteen litres, which the carter fills with wine before he leaves the Valtelline, to cheer him on the homeward journey. You raise it in both hands, and when the bung has been removed, allow the liquor to flow stream-wise down your throat. It was a most extraordinary Bacchic procession – a pomp which, though undreamed of on the banks of the Ilissus, proclaimed the deity of Dionysos in authentic fashion. Struggling horses, grappling at the ice-bound floor with sharp, spiked shoes; huge, hoarse drivers, some clad in sheepskins from Italian valleys, some brown as bears in rough Graubünden homespun; casks, dropping their spilth of red wine on the snow; greetings, embracings; patois of Bergamo, Romansch, and German roaring around the low-browed vaults and tingling ice pillars; pourings forth of libations of the new strong Valtelline on breasts and beards – the whole made up a scene of stalwart jollity and manful labour such as I have nowhere else in such wild circumstances witnessed. Many Davosers were there, the men of Andreas Gredig, Valär, and so forth; and all of these, on greeting Christian, forced us to drain a *Schluck* from their unmanageable cruses. Then on they went, crying, creaking, struggling, straining through the corridor, which echoed deafeningly, the gleaming crystals of those hard Italian mountains in their winter raiment building a background of still beauty to the savage Bacchanalian riot of the team.

How little the visitors who drink Valtelline wine at S. Moritz or Davos reflect by what strange ways it reaches them. A sledge can scarcely be laden with more than one cask of 300 litres on the ascent; and this cask, according to the state of the road, has many times to be shifted from wheels to runners and back again before the journey is accomplished. One carter will take charge of two horses, and consequently of two sledges and two casks, driving them both by voice and gesture rather than by rein. When they leave the Valtelline, the carters endeavour, as far as possible, to take the pass in gangs, lest bad weather or an accident upon the road should overtake them singly. At night they hardly rest three hours, and rarely think of sleeping, but spend the time in drinking and conversation. The horses are fed and littered; but for them too the night-halt is little better than a baiting-time. In fair weather the passage of the mountain is not difficult, though tiring. But woe to men and beasts alike if they encounter storms! Not a few perish in the passes; and it frequently happens that their only chance is to unyoke the horses and leave the sledges in a snow-wreath, seeking for themselves such shelter as may possibly be gained, frost bitten, after hours of battling with impermeable drifts. The wine is frozen into one solid mass of rosy ice before it reaches Pontresina. This does not hurt the young vintage, but it is highly injurious to wine of some years' standing. The perils of the journey are aggravated by the savage temper of the drivers. Jealousies between the natives of rival districts spring up; and there are men alive who have fought the whole way down from Fluela Hospice to Davos Platz with knives and stones, hammers and hatchets, wooden staves and splintered cart-wheels, staining the snow with blood, and bringing broken pates, bruised limbs, and senseless comrades home to their women to be tended.

Bacchus Alpinus shepherded his train away from us to northward, and we passed forth into noonday from the gallery. It then seemed clear that both conductor and postilion were sufficiently merry. The plunge they took us down those frozen parapets, with shriek and *jauchzen* and cracked whips, was more than ever dangerous. Yet we reached La Rosa safely. This is a lovely solitary spot, beside a rushing stream, among grey granite boulders grown with spruce and rhododendron: a veritable rose of Sharon blooming in the desert. The wastes of the Bernina stretch above, and round about are leaguered some of the most forbidding sharp-toothed peaks I ever saw. Onwards, across the silent snow, we glided in immitigable sunshine, through opening valleys and pine-woods, past the robber-huts of Pisciadella, until at evenfall we rested in the roadside inn at Poschiavo.

J A Symonds *Sketches and Studies in Italy and Greece,*1874

That is the most wonderful piece of descriptive writing to

which I can add nothing but admiration.

I have to confess to a total ignorance of Northern Italian wines, so I've had to do a little research. Very pleasant it was too. My recommendation is a bottle of Valtellina Superiore DOC, produced by Nino Negri.

Give me, give me Buriano,
Trebbiano, Colombano –
Give me bumpers, rich and clear!
'Tis the true old Aurum Potabile,
Gilding life when it wears shabbily:
Helen's old Nepenthe 'tis
That in the drinking
Swallowed thinking,
And was the receipt for bliss.
Thence it is, that ever and ay,
When he doth philosophize,
Good old glorious Rucellai
Hath it for light unto his eyes;
He lifteth it, and by the shine
Well discerneth things divine:
Atoms with their airy justles,
And all manner of corpuscles;
And, as through a crystal skylight,
How morning differeth from evening twilight;
And further telleth us the reason why go
Some stars with such a lazy light, and some with a vertigo.

O, how widely wandereth he,
Who in search of verity
Keeps aloof from glorious wine!
Lo, the knowledge it bringeth to me!
For Barbarossa, this wine so bright,
With its rich red look and its strawberry light,
So inviteth me,
So delighteth me,
I should infallibly quench my inside with it,
Had not Hippocrates
And old Andromachus
Strictly forbidden it
And loudly chidden it,
So many stomachs have sickened and died with it.
Yet, discordant as it is,
Two good biggins will not come amiss;
Because I know, while I'm drinking them down,
What is the finish and what is the crown.
A cup of good Corsican does it at once;
Or a glass of old Spanish
Is neat for the nonce:
Quackish resources are things for a dunce.

Talk of Chocolate!
Talk of Tea!
Medicines made – ye gods! – as they are,
Are no medicines made for me.
I would sooner take to poison
Than a single cup set eyes on
Of that bitter and guilty stuff ye
Talk of by the name of Coffee.
Let the Arabs and the Turks
Count it 'mongst their cruel works:
Foe of mankind, black and turbid,
Let the throats of slaves absorb it.
Down in Tartarus,
Down in Erebus,
'Twas the detestable Fifty invented it;
The Furies then took it
To grind and to cook it,
And to Proserpina all three presented it.
If the Mussulman in Asia
Doats on a beverage so unseemly,
I differ with the man extremely.

There's a squalid thing, called Beer:
The man whose lips that thing comes near
Swiftly dies; or falling foolish,
Grows, at forty, old and owlish.

She that in the ground would hide her,
Let her take to English Cider:
He who'd have his death come quicker,
 Any other Northern liquor.
Those Norwegians and those Laps
Have extraordinary tans
Those Laps especially have strange fancies;
To see them drink, I verily think,
Would make me lose my senses.
But a truce to such vile subjects,
With their impious, shocking objects.
Let me purify my mouth
In a holy cup o' th' South;
In a golden pitcher let me
Head and ears for comfort get me,
And drink of the wine of the vine benign
That sparkles warm in Sansovine.

Leigh Hunt from *Bacchus in Tuscany*, 1819

I do sometimes wish that I was much better read, for some
of the classical allusions in this delightful poem are beyond
me – hey ho.

Here's an unusual suggestion. It's a white wine from the
Chianti region of Tuscany, called Val d'Arbia made by Villa
Vistarenni.

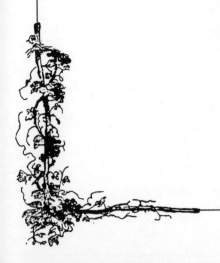

Now they set to to make the wine that is as necessary to their lives as bread and water. Behind the chapel and down a slope under some walnut trees is the *cantina,* the cellar, which is long and cool with a shallowly vaulted ceiling. Here the grapes are pressed and the wine kept in the huge oak barrels that line the walls. The tractor is driven round to the *cantina* and the cases unloaded, and the pressing of the grapes begins immediately. It is already dusk and the men work on into the night. The long room is lit by two dim light-bulbs dangling on dusty wires from the crumbling bricks, the walls are encrusted with aged dust and the cobwebbed barrels are immense in the shadows. The three men, Guido, Menchino and Tonio, watched by Sauro, move in the gloom operating the machinery like warlocks in some vast devil's kitchen. The shadows on their faces deepen in the faint light and if it were not for their clothes it would be difficult to put a date to the scene.

First they tip the cases of green grapes into a funnel-shaped apparatus outside the *cantina* wall, then they turn a handle like that of a mangle at the base of the funnel which half presses the fruit and sends the liquid and skins cascading through a window into a deep-walled stone trough inside the *cantina.* Here Tonio stirs the must with a long pole and rakes over the skins. This funnel-shaped machine, the *follatore,* is a simple form of the *égrappoir,* the machine used for the same purpose in more elaborate vineyards. The Cerottis' version has however no refinement to remove the stalks from the grapes, it is just a simple crushing device. The juice or must is filtered from the stone trough into the wooden vats through a large plastic pipe, the liquid sent on its way by a hand pump. The skins are then put into presses shaped like barrels with open slatted sides. A screw is turned at the top and this forces a plate down on to the skins, squeezing the remaining juice our between the side slats. A turgid yellow-green froth bubbles sluggishly from the base of the presses. This press wine, which is strong and full of tannin from the skins, is later added to the must in the fermenting barrels. The wrung-out skins, which some farmers use to make a rough *grappa,* in much the same way as French farmers make *marc,* are finally thrown out on to a field well away from the house as they would harm any poultry that ventured to eat them.

The black grapes are crushed in a separate machine and their must is put into an oak barrel together with the skins. The longer

123

the skins are left in the darker the wine will be. The wine will clarify, the sugar turning into alcohol, in about ten days' time, but the vats will remain unsealed for about a month in order to complete the fermentation. When this happens the barrels will be sealed properly with an air-tight clay seal to prevent the alcohol content of the wine dissipating and the wine turning to vinegar.

Elizabeth Romer *The Tuscan Year*, 1984

This is a timeless scene, evocatively and vividly described. We shouldn't pretend that modern wine-making techniques haven't done wonders for the industry, but it is still cheering to think that the simple skills that served wine-makers down the centuries haven't been entirely swept away by progress.

I think a bottle of 1990 Chianti Classico Assolo from the Villa Vistarenni would help me conjure up Tuscan memories.

Venice

The city on the lagoons is the next town to be considered, for Verona has scarcely a cuisine of its own, and Padua sends its best food to the Venetian market, and its Bagnoli wine as well. The Restaurant Quadri, on the north side of the Piazza of St Mark, is one of the best-known restaurants in Europe, and it is not expensive, for one can breakfast there well enough for 4 francs.

A gourmet of my acquaintance thus describes a typical breakfast at the Quadri. 'When you go to the restaurant do not be induced to go upstairs where the tourists are generally invited, but take a little table on the ground floor, where you can see all the piazza life, and begin with a *Vermouth Amaro*, in lieu of a 'cocktail'. For *hors-d'hœuvre* have some small crabs, cold, mashed up with *Sauce Tartare*, and perhaps a slice or two of *Presciutto Crudo*, raw ham cut as thin as cigarette-paper. After this a steaming *Risotto*, with *Scampe*, somewhat resembling gigantic prawns. Some cutlets done in Bologna style, a thin slice of ham on top and hot Parmesan and grated white truffles and *Fegato alla Veneziana* complete the repast, except for a slice of Strachino cheese. A bottle of Val Policella is exactly suited to this kind of repast, and a glass of fine-champagne (De Luze) for yourself and of ruby-coloured Alkermes for the lady, if your wife accompanies you, makes a good ending. The *maître-d'hôtel*, who looks like a retired ambassador, will be interested in you directly he finds that you know how a man should breakfast.'

Lt-Col Nathaniel Newnham-Davis and Algernon Bastard *The Gourmet's Guide to Europe*, 1903

And I presume they know how to lunch and dine as well. Messrs Newnham-Davis and Bastard probably weighed over fifty stone between them. I rather pity the 'lady'. According to Alexis Lichine, the 'ruby-coloured Alkermes' is a 'red cordial once made from the kermes insect of the cochineal genus'. The thought of a glass of Valpolicella is cheering, but be careful as most of it is rubbish.

No draught of wine amid the old tombs under the violet sky but made me for the time a better man, larger of brain, more courageous, more gentle . . . Could I but live for ever in thoughts and feelings such as those born to me in the shadow of the Italian vine!

George Gissing *The Private Papers of Henry Ryecroft,* 1903

Ah, noble sentiments! Though a word of caution, lest the 'feelings born to me in the shadow of the Italian vine' carry one away with unfortunate results.

I have not visited Italy often, but on one occasion I travelled almost its entire length, from Milan to Sicily. Two things struck me forcibly: the further south you go the more volatile the populace becomes and accompanying this there is an increasing reliance on gestures, the major conduit of communications. Thus the casual removal of a hair from the tip of your tongue, the rubbing between the forefinger and thumb of the bridge of the nose, the stroking of the right earlobe, all of which go unnoticed in Weybridge, are likely in Palermo to provoke unexpected assault from passers-by who think you're impugning their parentage.

So for goodness' sake look British. Always wear a tie south of Rome; south of Naples a two-piece suit and a bow tie (try to get hold of Garrick Club or MCC one, nobody but the English would mix such colours) and carry a furled parasol. In Sicily, regardless of season, there is only one answer: a three-piece pin-stripe suit, bowler hat and umbrella. You may be hot, but you will be unmolested.

Should you be caught in T-shirt, faded jeans, leather-thonged sandals and healthy suntan, for heaven's sake keep your hands by your sides when asking for something in a café, restaurant or shop. Adopt the most charming smile you can muster and speak slowly and very clearly. Thus, 'Una cappucino per favore,' should take about a minute to deliver. Never raise your voice; they tend to shout back.

I'm sure George Gissing would approve of a Barbaresco Sori San Lorenzo produced by Angelo Gaja. This is a particular favourite of Trevor Hughes and one he describes as 'a powerful, complex wine with great ageing ability'.

Why is it that Italian wines are so seldom featured on the wine lists of restaurants other than those which serve specifically Italian food? Italy produces a great variety, as well as a very large quantity of wines, and it does seem rather unimaginative to confine them to drinking entirely with Italian food. In the repertory of French regional and country cooking there are surely scores of dishes with which an authentic Italian wine would make a most refreshing change from the inevitable Beaujolais, and in fish restaurants especially, the too familiar and usually unidentifiable Chablis. Personally, I would welcome the occasional offer of a Verdicchio with the mussels, a fresh, light Frascati with the sole and spinach. And as far as the red wines are concerned, the lighter ones of Verona and Garda harmonize uncommonly well with pâtés, the fuller ones of Piedmont and Tuscany with *daubes* of beef, hot cheese dishes, rich ox-tail stews, game birds, herb-flavoured chickens.

Then for that matter, why not Italian wines with English food? We are, after all, more practised than are the people of wine-growing countries at the game of matching our dishes to appropriate wines. I have found that roast duck and a bottle of Piedmontese Barolo make a most excellent combination. And I think that a Barbera from the same region should do particularly well with a steak, kidney and mushroom pudding, or a jugged hare, while a Chianti Classico is a wine for roast lamb or a handsome joint of pork, as indeed it is in its native country, where the whole roast pigs, marvellously aromatic with wild fennel and whole garlic cloves roasted golden and translucent, are one of the most splendid features of Tuscan food markets. Impaled on a huge pole, the pig is carved to order, hefty slices, each with a portion of the golden garlic cloves scooped out from the inside, are handed to you with a big hunk of bread and wrapped in a paper napkin. The local housewives are buying it for the midday meal, but we are tourists, so we go off to another stall to buy cheese, perhaps a good big piece of Parmesan, finest of all cheeses with red wine. And we drive off, up into the beautiful Tuscan hills to find a picnic place in the warm autumn sun. We are worlds away from the baked lasagne, the veal with ham and mushrooms, the standard caramelized oranges and Bertorelli ices of everybody's Italian trattoria down the road. And although here in England we cannot hope to reproduce anything very close to true Italian country food (the ingredients are so elusive – where is the veal, where the good Parmesan, where the sweet, pale rose Parma ham, the fish straight out of the sea, the fruity Tuscan olive oil?) we can at least enjoy Italian wines and an increasingly large variety of them, without going to the local pizza house or trattoria, and with food of our own cooking and choosing. I do suggest too that these wines will benefit by being served with a shade less of that careless abandon which characterizes the Italian trattoria wine waiter. Open the red wines well in advance, don't chill the whites until they are as frozen as a sorbet.

For the pork dish, which I have chosen as being a good one with Italian red wine, I would settle for a flask of Chianti Classico Montepaldi, a very typical Chianti, clean and bright, not too heavy. A lighter wine, the delicious estate-bottled Lamberti Valpolicella from the Verona district would also be a happy choice. This wine incidentally is one which I would fancy for the Christmas turkey, while the full and fragrant red Torgiano from Umbria would be lovely with a roast fillet of beef, should anyone be rich enough for such a luxury this year. And for everyday drinking nobody should despise the much cheaper Tuscan red wine. It seems to me to offer remarkable value. But this wine too will improve noticeably if given an hour or two to breathe. At normal room temperature. *Not,* please not, in front of the fire. And the corner of the Aga is the place for the kettle, not for the red wine.

Elizabeth David *An Omelette and a Glass of Wine,* 1984

Elizabeth David is one of the writers on wine for whom I have most regard. Although she was not primarily a wine writer, when she wrote about the wines of a region she showed exactly the same magic ability to conjure up flavour, fragrance and ambiance which made her the world's most innovative cookery writer. Here she combines her expertise in both fields with mouth-watering effect.

To complement her call for a little imagination for Italian wines I'd like to propose a bottle of Donna Guilia, Méthode Champenoise, Brut Rosé, produced in the vineyards of La Terrazze on the Adriatic coast of Italy. The Italians rave about it: now it's our turn to share their enjoyment.

The Germans are exceedingly fond of Rhine wines: they are put up in tall, slender bottles, and are considered a pleasant beverage. One tells them from vinegar by the label.

Mark Twain *A Tramp Abroad* 1880, 1982

And, I hope, by taste. German wines are another gap in my knowledge. I've tasted a Rhine wine called Niersteiner Pettenthal, Riesling Auslese, grown by Balbach. It was spicy but wonderfully mellow.

I made acquaintance also with Mr Christopher Smith, a very old wine merchant, who told me that when he had come to a state of manhood (about the year 1750), and drinking wine at taverns, it was eightpence per quart, served up in a curious pewter measure, which turned round upon a little swivel, with a spout, and, if ten were in company, one glass served them all. The call was only for red wine or white wine, but frequently the red was called claret, and the white sherry. *Sherry was then generally, like other white wines, kept in state of fermentation, by sweet malaga, meade, cider, or honey.* Pale wine was but just coming home (about 1768) on the lees, with which was mixed Spanish or small French wine; and a similar mixture was made of the various sorts of white wines. The dexterity of the wine cooper then was shown in making the most palatable at the lowest prices; but now (referring to 1807, the date of his letter) all wine comes in so clean and so perfect that the skill of the wine cooper of former days is not required. With white port, being subject to ferment in summer and grow foul in winter, we mixed a little Teneriffe, which improved its flavour, and prevented any further fermentation.

I think three years had elapsed before I had seen a butt of sherry; but when I did, I recommended it in preference to white port. A man of quality recommended to me Mr Duff, our late consul at Cadiz, to whom I sent orders from several friends, and white port soon became despised, although it had been in such esteem that, even as late as 1782, I got orders in one week for eighty pipes. Now it is forgotten, and sherry has prevailed.

From a letter quoted in Thomas George Shaw's *The Wine, the Vine and the Cellar*, 1863

When I was about eighteen or nineteen I was walking down the street in Highgate where my parents lived when a charming neighbour of theirs, whose name shamefully eludes me, asked whether I'd like a glass of sherry. 'Certainly,' I said and so we sat down to our first glass and rose some time later having consumed most of three bottles. I have never had such a hangover: it took three days to clear!

I have not drunk sherry from that day until this afternoon

when. for the sake of this book, I took a glass of chilled Tio Pepe from Gonzalez Byass. I'm afraid I only managed a sip or two before some lightning conductor between the taste buds and liver sent a 26-year-old instruction to my brain. 'Stop now,' it said, 'or you'll be in deep trouble.'

But fear not, dear reader, I have quite vivid teenage memories of sherry and if I run out of suggestions, I'll tell you more stories about the man I'm about to mention. But for the moment you stick to your Tio Pepe and I'll stick to mine.

When the late and very great Sir Ralph Richardson was a young and successful actor he drank champagne every day of his life. He even had his own label printed 'Cuvée Ralph Richardson' for his favourite. Then one morning he woke up and thought, 'I never want to taste champagne again for as long as I live.' I worked with him when he was seventy and he hadn't tasted champagne for forty years. His post-performance drink was gin, but more of that later.

An invitation to 'come over for a glass of sherry' promises a relaxed communion of friends, of comfortable shoes, an old sweater, an occasion that no one will be using as part of life's strategic game plan.

Gerald Asher On Wine

And a three-day hangover! The sherry I was drinking that notorious afternoon was a traditional Amontillado. This is rich and dark in colour, but dry in taste - quite wonderful, in moderation.

Answer of Ale to the Challenge of Sack

Come all you brave wights,
That are dubbed ale-knights,
   Now set out yourselves in sight;
And let them that crack
In the presence of Sack
   Know Malt is of mickle might.

Though Sack they define
Is holy divine,
     Yet it is but naturall liquor,
Ale hath for its part
An addition of art
     To make it drinke thinner or thicker.

Sack; fiery fume,
Doth waste and consume
     Men's humidum radicale;
It scaldeth their livers,
It breeds burning feavers,
     Proves vinum venenum reale.

But history gathers,
From aged forefathers,
     That Ale's the true liquor of life,
Men lived long in health,
And preserved their wealth,
     Whilst Barley broth only was rife.

Sack, quickly ascends,
And suddenly ends,
     What company came for at first,
And that which yet worse is,
It empties men's purses
     Before it half quenches their thirst.

Ale, is not so costly
Although that the most lye
     Too long by the oyle of Barley;
Yet may they part late,
At a reasonable rate,
     Though they came in the morning early.

Sack, makes men from words
Fall to drawing of swords,
        And quarrelling endeth their quaffing;
Whilst dagger ale Barrels
Beare off many quarrels .
        And often turn chiding to laughing.

Sack's drink for our masters,
All may be Ale-tasters,
        Good things the more common the better,
Sack's but single broth,
Ale's meat, drinke, and cloathe,
        Say they that know never a letter.

But not to entangle
Old friends till they wrangle
        And quarrell for other men's pleasure;
Let Ale keep his place,
        And let Sack have his grace,
        So that neither exceed the due measure.

Francis Beaumont 1584–1616

I particularly like 'Good things the more common the better'.

An occasional half of bitter I find very pleasant and here in East Anglia I have a favourite called Abbot Ale. It is delicious in taste and, be warned, very strong. You can find it in other parts of the country, but not easily. Try some.

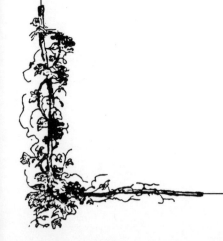

One might jangle a long time on Montillas and Olorosos, Amorosos and the so vilely traduced Vino de Pasto itself; one might, perhaps, give a friendly hint to an ingenuous writer, such as those who think 'Carte d'Or' a special brand of champagne, that 'Solera' is not a particular *kind* of sherry. The Spanish wine merchants, or their English clients, have, moreover, a pretty taste for giving feminine names to this wine. My cellars (and even cupboards) have seldom for forty years been without a certain 'Margarita', from some vaults in 'Bristol cit*ee*', which were originally recommended to me by an actual Margaret, its namesake and fellow-citizen; and an 'Emilia', an 'Isabel' and a 'Maria' (more than one, indeed, for there is a *Tia* Maria, to match the Tio Pepe) have kept her company at various times without quarrel or jealousy. Even a 'Titania' appears in my book. But these are fantasies.

George Saintsbury *Notes on a Cellar-Book,* 1920

My last sherry suggestion is that you try a Manzanilla. I say this because I remember the name from my youth; I think my grandfather drank it. I can't remember the taste, but my wine merchant friend tells me it's dry and he recommends Manzilla La Gitana, made by Hidalgo.

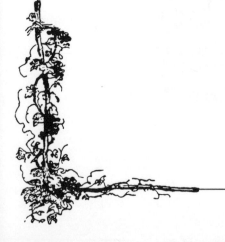

To produce black strong and rich wine, the following are the expedients resorted to: The grapes being flung into the open vat indiscriminately with the stalks, sound and unsound, are trodden by men till they are completely smashed, and then left to ferment. When the wine is about half fermented it is transferred from the vat to tonels; and brandy (several degrees above proof) is thrown in, in the proportion of twelve to twenty-five gallons to the pipe of must, by which the fermentation is generally checked. About two months afterwards, this mixture is coloured thus: a quantity of dried elderberries is put into coarse bags; these are placed in vats, and a part of the wine to be coloured being thrown over them, they are trodden by men till the whole of the colouring matter is expressed, when the husks are thrown away. The dye thus formed, is applied according to the fancy of the owner, from twenty-eight to fifty-six pounds of the dried elderberries being used to the pipe of wine! Another addition of brandy, of from four to six gallons per pipe, is now made to the mixture, which is then allowed to rest for about two months. At the end of this time it is, if sold, sent to Villa Nova, where it is racked two or three times; and receives probably two gallons more of brandy per pipe, and it is then considered fit to be shipped to England, it being about nine months old. At the time of shipment one gallon more of brandy is usually added to each pipe. The wine thus having received at least twenty gallons of brandy per pipe, is considered by the merchant sufficiently strong.

Thomas George Shaw *The Wine, the Vine, and the Cellar*, 1863

(A pipe contains 105 Imperial gallons.)
   A good vintage port is a delicious end to a meal, the last one I tried was Warres 1975, bottled in '77 – very good.

140

That Port should follow Sherry is, or ought to be, to any decent Englishman, a thing requiring no argument. My cellar, if not exactly my cellar-book (which, as has been said, did not begin till some years later), was founded in this eminent respect on a small supply of 1851 (I think, but am not sure, Cockburn's), whereof my friend in Pall Mall, but from Scotland, who supplied it, ingenuously said that for his part he liked rich port, but that for a medium dry wine he did not think it could be surpassed. Nor have I, to my remembrance, ever drunk much better than this, or than some magnums of the same shippers and vintage which succeeded it, and were bought at the sale of that air-travelling victim, Mr Powell, of Wiltshire. Indeed, I think '51 was the finest port, of what may be called the older vintages accessible to my generation, that I ever tasted; it was certainly the finest that I ever possessed. The much talked of 1820 I do not think that I ever drank *securus,* that is to say, under circumstances which assured its being genuine. Some '34, with such a guarantee, I have drunk, and more '47, the latter from when it was about in perfection (say, in 1870) to a date the other day when it was some sixty years old and little but a memory, or at least a suggestion. But '51 in all its phases, dry, rich and medium, was, I think, such a wine as deserved the famous and pious encomium (slightly altered) that the Almighty might no doubt have caused a better wine to exist, but that he never did.

For some years, however, after the book was started I did not drink much port, being in the heat of my devotion to Claret or Burgundy after dinner. I cannot find that I ever possessed any '54, which, though not a large or very famous vintage, some not bad judges ranked with '51 itself, but I have records of '58, '61, of course '63, '68, '70, '72, '75 and '78 in the first division of my book, and before the interval in which I did not keep it regularly. During that interval I was accused and convicted of acute rheumatism, and sentenced, as usual, to give up port altogether – which was all the harder as I had just returned to my natural allegiance thereto. The result was that several dozens of what was going to be one of the best wines of the century, Dow's '78, comforted the sick and afflicted of a Cambridgeshire village; and that the only 'piece' of port that I ever laid down – a quarter-cask of Sandeman's '81 – was taken back on very generous terms by the merchants who had supplied it. They gave me an additional five per cent per annum on what I had given for it.

However, other people had to be provided for, and I did not myself practise total abstinence. I seem, from menus preserved, though the book was in suspense, to have trusted chiefly to three kinds, no one of which perhaps would have been highly esteemed by a person who went by common opinion, but which had merits. One was a wine of uncertain vintage, believed to be '53, and probably Sandeman's, but certainly very good. Another was a Rebello Valente of '65. Now '65, like '53, has no *general* repute as a vintage, and some people think Rebello Valente 'coarse.' I can only say that this, for a 'black-strap' wine, was excellent, and I confess that I do not despise 'black-strap'. But the gem of the three was a '73 which had been allowed to remain in wood till it was eight or nine years old, and in bottle for about as much longer before I bought it. It had lost very little colour and not much body of the best kind; but if there ever was any devil in its soul that soul had thoroughly exorcised the intruder and replaced him with an angel. I had my headquarters at Reading at the time, and a member of my family was being attended by the late Mr Oliver Maurice, one of the best-known practitioners between London and Bristol. He once appeared rather doubtful when I told him that I had given his patient port; so I made him taste this. He drank it as port should be drunk – a trial of the bouquet; a slow sip; a rather larger and slightly less slow one, and so on; but never a gulp; and during the drinking his face exchanged its usual bluff and almost brusque aspect for the peculiar blandness – a blandness as of Beulah if not of Heaven itself – which good wine gives to worthy countenances. And when he set the glass down he said, softly but cordially, '*That* won't do her any harm.' But I am not entirely certain that in his heart of hearts he did not think it rather wasted on a lady, in which, as I have said, *I* think he was wrong.

George Saintsbury *Notes on a Cellar-Book,* 1920

The oldest bottle of port I have ever drunk was a 1948 Cockburn's – wonderful.

Sheridan was dining with Lord Thurlow, when his Lordship produced some fine Constantia, which had been sent to him from the Cape of Good Hope. The wine tickled the palate of Sheridan, who saw the bottle emptied with uncommon regret, and set his wits to work to get another. The old Chancellor was not to be so easily induced to produce his curious Cape in such profusion, and foiled all attempts to get another glass. Sheridan, being piqued, and seeing the inutility of persecuting the immovable pillar of the law, turned towards a gentleman seated further down, and said, 'Sir, pass me up that decanter; for I must return to Madeira, since I cannot double the Cape.'

John Timbs (1801-1875) *A Century of Anecdote*

Sheridan is, of course, the man who, when encountered having a drink while watching his theatre, Drury Lane, burn to the ground, said, 'A man may surely be allowed to take a glass of wine by his own fireside.'

I was brought up in a household where any South African produce was strictly forbidden. So it is only in the last few years that I have tasted South African wines. I have discovered that the Groot Constantia estate includes the original Constantia Farm. So if we try the Gewürztraminer from Groot Constantia we may well be drinking the wine that Sheridan so enjoyed.

from How Pleasant to Know Mr Lear

He sits in a beautiful parlour,
With hundreds of books on the wall:
He drinks a great deal of Marsala,
But never gets tipsy at all.

Edward Lear *c.*1875

I'm not sure that I've ever tasted Marsala on its own, but I often order zabaglione as a pudding in Italian restaurants. So a foaming glass of slightly warm, pale yellow zabaglione for the great Mr Lear.

Solomon looked a little graver as he finished his dinner, and glanced from time to time at the boy's bright face. When dinner was done, and the cloth was cleared away (the entertainment had been brought from a neighbouring eating-house), he lighted a candle, and went down below into a little cellar, while his nephew, standing on the mouldy staircase, dutifully held the light. After a moment's groping here and there, he presently returned with a very ancient-looking bottle, covered with dust and dirt.

'Why, Uncle Sol!' said the boy, 'what are you about! that's the wonderful Madeira – there's only one more bottle!'

Uncle Sol nodded his head, implying that he knew very well what he was about; and having drawn the cork in solemn silence, filled two glasses and set the bottle and a third clean glass on the table.

'You shall drink the other bottle, Wally,' he said, 'when you have come to good fortune; when you are a thriving, respected, happy man; when the start in life you have made to-day shall have brought you, as I pray Heaven it may! – to a smooth part of the course you have to run, my child. My love to you!'

Some of the fog that hung about old Sol seemed to have got into his throat; for he spoke huskily. His hand shook too, as he clinked his glass against his nephew's. But having once got the wine to his lips, he tossed it off like a man, and smacked them afterwards.

'Dear Uncle,' said the boy, affecting to make light of it, while the tears stood in his eyes, 'for the honour you have done me, et cetera, et cetera. I shall now beg to propose Mr Solomon Gills with three times three and one cheer more. Hurrah! and you'll return thanks, Uncle, when we drink the last bottle together; won't you?'

They clinked their glasses again; and Walter, who was hoarding his wine, took a sip of it, and held the glass up to his eye with as critical an air as he could possibly assume . . . Solomon Gills rubbed his hands with an air of stealthy enjoyment, as he talked of the sea, though; and looked on the seafaring objects about him with inexpressible complacency.

'Think of this wine for instance,' said old Sol, 'which has been to the East Indies and back, I'm not able to say how often, and has been once round the world. Think of the pitch-dark nights, the roaring winds, and rolling seas.'

'The thunder, lightning, rain, hail, storm of all kinds,' said the boy.

'To be sure,' said Solomon, ' – that this wine has passed through. Think what a straining and creaking of timbers and masts: what a whistling and howling of the gale through ropes and rigging.'

'What a clambering aloft of men, vying with each other who shall lie out first upon the yards to furl the icy sails, while the ship rolls and pitches, like mad!' cried his nephew.

'Exactly so,' said Solomon: 'has gone on, over the old cask that held this wine. Why, when the Charming Sally went down in the—'

'In the Baltic Sea, in the dead of night; five-and-twenty minutes past twelve when the captain's watch stopped in his pocket; he lying dead against the main-mast – on the fourteenth of February, seventeen forty-nine!' cried Walter, with great animation.

'Aye, to be sure!' cried old Sol, 'quite right! Then, there were five hundred casks of such wine aboard; and all hands (except the first mate, first lieutenant, two seamen, and a lady, in a leaky boat) going to work to stave the casks, got drunk and died drunk, singing "Rule Britannia", when she settled and went down, and ending with one awful scream in chorus.'

Charles Dickens *Dombey and Son*, 1847-8

My wine merchant Trevor Hughes has in his current list a 1789 vintage Sercial Teixeira. But hurry, there's only one bottle left . . . £600 plus VAT.

BRANDY, n. A cordial composed of one part thunder-and-lightning, one part remorse, two parts bloody murder, one part death-hell-and-the-grave, two parts clarified Satan and four parts holy Moses! Dose, a headful all the time. Brandy is said, by Emerson, I think, to be the drink of heroes. I certainly should not advise others to tackle it.

Ambrose Bierce *The Enlarged Devil's Dictionary* ed E J Hopkins, 1971

I used to drink cognac quite a lot. I had some wonderful Hine 1962, pale gold in colour with an incredibly rich taste. Now I find it too strong and it always gives me a hangover. But just occasionally late on a hot summer's night a glass of cognac, ice and soda is the perfect nightcap.

Inviting a Friend to Supper

Tonight, grave sir, both my poor house and I,
    Do equally desire your company:
Not that we think us worthy such a guest,
    But that your worth will dignify our feast,
With those that come; whose grace may make that seem
    Something, which, else, could hope for no esteem.
It is the fair acceptance, Sir, creates
    The entertainment perfect: not the cates.
Yet shall you have, to rectify your palate,
    An olive, capers, or some better salad
Ushering the mutton; with a short-legged hen,
    If we can get her, full of eggs, and then,
Lemons, and wine for sauce: to these, a coney
    Is not to be despaired of, for our money;
And, though fowl, now, be scarce, yet there are clerks,
    The sky not falling, think we may have larks.
I'll tell you of more, and lie, so you will come:
    Of partridge, pheasant, wood-cock, of which some
May yet be there; and godwit, if we can:
    Knat, rail, and ruff too. How so e'er, my man
Shall read a piece of VIRGIL, TACITUS,
    LIVY, or of some better book to us,
Of which we'll speak our minds, amidst our meat;
    And I'll profess no verses to repeat:
To this, if ought appear, which I know not of,
    That will the pastry, not my paper, show of.
Digestive cheese, and fruit there sure will be;
    But that, which most doth take my *Muse,* and me,
Is a pure cup of rich *Canary*-wine,
    Which is the *Mermaid's,* now, but shall be mine:
Of which had HORACE, or ANACREON tasted,
    Their lives, as do their lines, till now had lasted.
Tobacco, Nectar, or the *Thespian* spring,
    Are all but LUTHER'S beer, to this I sing.
Of this we will sup free, but moderately,
    And we will have no *Pooly* or *Parrot* by;

Nor shall our cups make any guilty men.
But, at our parting, we will be, as when
We innocently met. No simple word,
That shall be uttered at our mirthful board,
Shall make us sad next morning: or affright
The liberty, that we'll enjoy to-night.

Ben Jonson, 1616

The Canary wine Jonson mentions is another name for sack, which we now know as sherry – so another Ralph Richardson story.

As I've said, the play I was in with Sir Ralph was at the Savoy Theatre, tucked down the side of the Savoy Hotel. After every Wednesday matinée Ralph would have bangers and mash sent down to his dressing-room from the hotel kitchen. To the bewilderment of the front stalls he would take his curtain call at the matinée chanting 'sausages, sausages' at almost full volume.

Return visits to Oxford were always a cause of celebration for Parson Woodforde who indulged both his gastronomic and his intellectual appetites to the full. Here he is enjoying the best his college had to offer in the summer of 1774.

July 27. I breakfasted, dined, supped and slept again at College. Cooke Senr, and Master Senr, breakfasted with me. I sent a note to Mr Bowerbank of Queen's this morning to desire him to dine with me to-day, which he will.

Gave Bull's Boy Gooby, this morning, 0. 0. 6. Mr Hindley, Dr Thurlowe, Master of the Temple, Dr Burrows, Dr Birchenden, and Mr Bowerbank dined and spent the afternoon with me at New College. I borrowed the Chequer Room of the Bursars for my company to dine in. We were very merry and pushed the Bottle on very briskly. I gave my Company for dinner, some green Pea Soup, a chine of Mutton, some New College Puddings, a goose, some Peas and a Codlin Tart with Cream. Madeira and Port Wine to drink after and at dinner some strong Beer, Cyder, Ale and small Beer. Dr West spent part of the afternoon and supped and spent the evening with me. I had a handsome dish of fruit after dinner. At 7 o'clock we all went from the Chequer to my Room where we had Coffee and Tea. Dr Birchenden went from us soon after coffee and did not return again . . . . Mr Hindley, Dr Thurlowe, Dr West, Dr Burrows and Mr Bowerbank, supped and stayed with me till after one. Mr Hindley, Dr Burrows, Mr Bowerbank and myself got to Cards after coffee. At whist I won 1. 0. 6 out of which, Mr Hindley owes me 0. 5. 0. I gave my company only for supper cold mutton. After supper I gave them to drink some Arrac Punch with Jellies in it and some Port wine. I made all my Company but Dr West quite merry. We drank 8 bottles of Port one Bottle of Madeira besides Arrac Punch, Beer and Cyder. I carried off my drinking exceedingly well indeed.

The Revd James Woodforde (1758-1802) *The Diary of a Country Parson*

What was wrong with Dr West? Was he teetotal, seriously ill or just very depressed? Poor man, we shall never know.

'Cyder' is a drink we haven't talked about yet. My

favourite is the almost pink cider from Normandy, which is becoming readily available now in this country.

When Lord Sparkish, Tom Neverout, and Colonel Allwit, the immortal personages of Swift's polite conversation, came to breakfast with my Lady Smart, at eleven o'clock in the morning, my Lord Smart was absent at the levée. His Lordship was at home to dinner at three o'clock to receive his guests; and we may sit down to this meal like the Barmecides's, and see the fops of the last century before us. Seven of them sat down at dinner, and were joined by a country baronet who told them they kept court hours. These persons of fashion began their dinner with a sirloin of beef, fish, a shoulder of veal, and a tongue. My Lady Smart carved the sirloin, my Lady Answerall helped the fish and the gallant Colonel cut the shoulder of veal. All made a considerable inroad on the sirloin and the shoulder of veal, with the exception of Sir John, who had no appetite, having already partaken of a beefsteak and two mugs of ale, besides a tankard of March beer as soon as he got out of bed. They drank claret, which the Master of the house said should always be drunk after fish; and my Lord Smart particularly recommended some excellent cider to my Lord Sparkish, which occasioned some brilliant remarks from that nobleman. When the host called for wine, he nodded to one or other of his guests, and said 'Tom Neverout, my service to you.'

After the first course came almond-pudding, fritters, which the Colonel took with his hands out of the dish, in order to help the brilliant Miss Notable; chickens, black puddings, and soup; and the Lady Smart, the elegant mistress of the mansion, finding a skewer in a dish, placed it in her plate, with directions that it should be carried down to the cook and dressed for the cook's own dinner. Wine and small beer were drunk during this second course; and when the Colonel called for beer, he called the butler Friend, and asked whether the beer was good. Various jocular remarks passed from the gentlefolk to the servants; at breakfast several persons had a word and a joke for Mrs. Betty, my lady's maid, who warmed the cream and had charge of the canister (the tea cost thirty shillings a pound in those days). When my Lady Sparkish sent her footman out to my Lady Match to come at six o'clock and play at quadrille, her ladyship warned the man to follow his nose, and if he fell by the way, not to stay to get up again. And when the gentleman asked the hall-porter if his lady was at home, that functionary replied, with manly waggishness, 'She was at home just now but she's not gone out yet.'

After the pudding, sweet and black, the fritters and soup, came the third course, of which the chief dish was a hot venison pasty, which was put before Lord Smart, and carved by that nobleman. Besides the pasty, there was a hare, a rabbit, some pigeons, partridge, a goose, and a ham. Beer and wine were freely imbibed during this course, the gentlemen always pledging somebody, with every glass which they drank; and by this time the conversation between Tom Neverout and Miss Notable had grown so brisk and lively, that the Derbyshire baronet began to think the young gentlewoman was Tom's sweetheart; on which Miss remarked, that she loved Tom 'like pie'. After the goose, some of the gentlemen took a dram of brandy, 'which was very good for the wholesomes,' Sir John said; and now having had a tolerably substantial dinner, honest Lord Smart bade the butler bring up the great tankard full of October to Sir John. The great tankard was passed from hand to hand and mouth to mouth, but when pressed by the noble host upon the gallant Tom Neverout, he said, 'No, faith, my lord, I like your wine, and won't put a churl upon a gentleman. Your honour's claret is good enough for me.' And so, the dinner over, the host said, 'Hang saving, bring us up a ha'porth of cheese . . .'

The cloth was now taken away, and a bottle of Burgundy was set down, of which the ladies were invited to partake before they went to their tea. When they withdrew, the gentlemen promised to join them in an hour: fresh bottles were brought; the 'dead men' meaning the empty bottles, removed; and 'd'you hear, John? bring clean glasses,' my lord Smart said. On which the gallant Colonel Allwit said, 'I'll keep my glass; for wine is the best liquor to wash glasses in.'

William Makepeace Thackeray *The Four Georges*, 1855-6

I'm not sure I approve of these people, particularly their attitude to the servants. Their modern counterparts are those groups of moneyed young people who sometimes frequent the smarter London eateries. They are deliberately arrogant and/or patronizing towards the staff, and always end up throwing bits of bread at each other.

Back to my beloved Burgundy. Try a bottle of Hautes Côtes de Beaune Clos de la Perrière, Domaine Guillemard Pothier.

I will give you, dear reader, an account of a dinner I have ordered this very day at Lovegrove's at Blackwall . . . The party will consist of seven men beside myself, and every guest is asked for some reason – upon which good fellowship mainly depends, for people brought together unconnectedly had, in my opinion, better be kept separate . . .

The dinner is to consist of turtle followed by no other fish but whitebait, which is to be followed by no other meat but grouse, which are to be succeeded simply by apple fritters and jelly, pastry on such occasions being quite out of place. With the turtle of course there will be punch, with the whitebait, champagne, and with the grouse, claret . . . I shall permit no other wines, unless perchance a bottle of port . . . With respect to the adjuncts, I shall take care that there is cayenne, with lemon cut in halves, not in quarters, within reach of everyone, for the turtle, and that brown bread and butter in abundance is set upon the table for the whitebait. It is no trouble to think of these little matters beforehand, but they make a vast difference in convivial contentment. The dinner will be followed by ices and a good dessert, and after which, coffee and one glass of liqueur each and no more; so that the present may be enjoyed rationally without introducing retrospective regrets. If the master of a feast wishes his party to succeed he must know how to command, and not let his guests run riot each according to his own wild fancy. Such, reader, is my idea of a dinner, of which I hope you approve.

Thomas Walker *The Original*, 1835

With a headmaster of a host, woe betide anyone who wants cayenne and lemon juice on his whitebait! I'm inclined to letting my guests 'run riot each according to his own wild fancy' – it's much more fun.

'With the turtle of course there will be punch' – little wonder the consumption of punch at mealtimes has declined since Walker's day.

Some rum punches are delicious, particularly Planter's Punch. But I find they are never quite as good here as those in the sunny islands of their origin. The same, of course, goes for retsina; different and intriguing on a sunny Greek island, like drinking furniture polish in London.

Upon such occasions poor Mr Woodhouse's feelings were in sad warfare. He loved to have the cloth laid, because it had been the fashion of his youth; but his conviction of suppers being very unwholesome made him rather sorry to see anything put on it; and while his hospitality would have welcomed his visitors to everything, his care for their health made him grieve that they would eat.

Such another small basin of gruel as his own was all that he could, with thorough self-approbation, recommend, though he might constrain himself, while the ladies were comfortably clearing the nicer things, to say:

'Mrs Bates, let me propose your venturing on one of these eggs. An egg boiled very soft is not unwholesome. Serle understands boiling an egg better than anybody. I would not recommend an egg boiled by anybody else – but you need not be afraid – they are very small, you see – one of our small eggs will not hurt you. Miss Bates, let Emma help you to a *little* bit of tart – a *very* little bit. Ours are all apple tarts. You need not be afraid of unwholesome preserves here. I do not advise the custard. Mrs Goddard, what do you say to *half* a glass of wine? A *small* half glass – put into a tumbler of water? I do not think it could disagree with you.'

Jane Austen *Emma*, 1816

I can hear Mr Woodhouse's thin reedy voice and his pedantic pause-filled delivery – beautiful writing. 'A *small* half glass of wine – put into a tumbler of water?' – an early example of the now extinct flat spritzer.

Spritzers are more difficult to make refreshing than you think. You need a cheap white wine that has some acidity. I find an inexpensive Muscadet de Sèvre-et-Maine fits the bill well.

In helping a lady to wine, *always* fill the glass to the very brim, for custom prevents them from taking many glasses at a time; and I have seen cross looks when the rule has been neglected by young and inexperienced dandies.

Sir Morgan O'Doherty, Bart *Maxims*

A custom that I *think* may be on the decline.

What shall we fill the lady's glass with? I know, a glass of delicious demi-sec Anjou Rosé called Château d'Auville.

Dinner at the Huntercombes' possessed only two dramatic features
– the wine was a farce and the food a tragedy.

Anthony Powell *The Acceptance World*, 1955

A wine that is certainly not farcical but has an unusual name
is Beaune Clos des Mouches. Now 'clos' means a walled
vineyard and 'mouches' are flies. It loses something in
translation, doesn't it?

A friend of mine at a restaurant in the South of France,
unexpectedly coming across a couple that he'd done business
with, asked how long they were staying.

'Most of the summer,' drawled the woman. 'We own a
villa on Cap d'Ail.'

'Ah,' said my friend, 'Garlic Point, I know it well.'

The 'ancient' banquets described here were actually those enjoyed in Tudor England . . .

In enumerating the luxuries of the ancient banquet, it must not be supposed that wine, that requisite of convivial scenes, was wanting to complete its allurements. We have seen in what profusion the Rhenish wines were distributed to the multitudes who thronged to view the festivities of the Court, on various public occasions; and it may easily be supposed how common the use of such an article must have been, to have authorized so liberal a distribution to the populace. The consumption of wine, although prodigious, appears, however, to have been regulated in the houses of our nobility and monarchs with scrupulous attention to economy, notwithstanding the low value of those most in general use. Henry VIII bestowed considerable attention upon the article of wine, and by several statutes endeavoured to restrain the increased prices of 'Malmsey, romaneis, or rumney, sack, and other sweet wines'.

The wines most in use at this period appear to have been Malmsey, Rhenish, and the wines of Gascony and of Guienne; which last were introduced into England at the time when part of the French dominions surrendered to the British arms; besides these, it has been decided that the champagne vintage was already in great repute; and among others who estimated its productions,

Henry VIII is numbered, and is even stated to have held one of the vineyards of Ay in his own hands; sack, that still unexplained object of antiquarian inquiry, was also one of the luxuries of this age.

At coronations or banquets it was, however, invariably the custom to dilute the genuine wines, and to cover the harshness and acidity which they possessed by mixing them with honey or with spices. 'Thus compounded,' says a modern writer on the subject, 'they passed under the generic name of piments, because they were originally prepared by the *pigmentarii* or apothecaries, and they were used much in the same manner as the *liqueurs* of modern times. The varieties of piment chiefly introduced at the banquets of our kings were hippocras, so called from the bag termed 'Hippocrates' sleeve', through which it was strained; and clarry, or clarre, a claret, or mixed wine, mingled with honey, and frequently drunk as a composing draught by persons who were on the point of retiring to rest. These beverages, especially hippocras, were deemed too expensive to be distributed on ordinary occasions, nor do they appear from the accounts given by our chroniclers to have been presented more than once during the feast. Metheglin or mead, braket, a composition of ale and honey, a very ancient drink in this country, and ale, were chiefly used for private persons and domestics.

F W Hackwood *Good Cheer,* 1911

Here I think we may see one of the reasons why we are not really a wine-drinking nation (except for champagne). If even the wines dispensed on special occasions needed mixing with honey or spices to mask their harshness and acidity, then why bother? Wouldn't it be better to stick to mead and ale? I think on a cold winter's evening a glass of strong ale, say a barley wine, with a small amount of liquid honey stirred into it might be very restorative!

Writing in 1911, Hackwood describes the order of serving wine familiar to Edwardian diners in contrast to the 'reign of Philistinism' from the early years of the preceding century.

By general gastronomic consent the usual order of wines at dinner is to offer a glass of light pale sherry or dry Sauterne after the soup; a delicate Rhine wine if required after fish; a glass of good Bordeaux with the joint of mutton; the same, or dry Champagne, during the *entrées;* the best of red wines, Bordeaux or Burgundy, with the roast game. With the dessert a full-flavoured but matured Champagne or a liqueur may be served.

This is the orthodox rule for a really good family meal. But the *bon vivant* does not restrict himself to so simple a list of dinner beverages as this. He will take Chablis with the oysters, sherry with soup, one glass of good Rhine wine with the fish, Champagne with the *entrées* and removes, a choice claret or Burgundy with the roast, and with the dessert will wind up with one glass of glorious port, 'king of wines'.

In the reign of Philistinism, which prevailed some seventy or eighty years ago, a host of the old school [Thomas Walker, quoted on page 155] said to his guests at the outset of the dinner: 'With the turtle there will be punch; champagne and claret afterwards; the two former I have ordered to be well iced. I shall permit no other wines, unless perchance a bottle or two of port, as I hold variety of wines to be a great mistake.'

F W Hackwood Good Cheer

A well-known and quite elderly character actor went on a twelve-week tour of the UK. At the end of the second week he went to the company manager and said, 'I wonder if next week my dressing-room could be at stage level, because I tend to drink rather a lot during the show and the stairs are becoming increasingly difficult.'

Try a dry white port. Churchill's make a good one.

According to Leigh Hunt, Oliver Goldsmith owed the inspiration for *She Stoops to Conquer* to a bizarre episode of mistaken hospitality.

It has been said that Goldsmith's comedy of *She Stoops to Conquer*, originated in the following adventure of the author. Some friend had given the young poet a guinea, when he left his mother's residence at Ballymahon, for a school in Edgworth's Town, where, it appears, he finished his education. He had diverted himself by viewing the gentlemen's seats on the road, until night-fall, when he found himself a mile or two out of the direct road, in the middle of the streets of Ardagh. Here he inquired for the best house in the place, meaning an inn; but a fencing-master, named Kelly, wilfully misunderstanding him, directed him to the large old-fashioned residence of Sir Ralph Featherstone, as the landlord of the town. There he was shown into the parlour, and found the hospitable master of the house sitting by a good fire. His mistake was immediately perceived by Sir Ralph, who being a man of humour, and well acquainted with the poet's family, encouraged him in the deception. Goldsmith ordered a good supper, invited his host and the family to partake of it, treated them to a bottle or two of wine, and, on going to bed, ordered a hot cake for his breakfast; nor was it until his departure, when he called for his bill, that he discovered that, while he imagined he was at an inn, he had been hospitably entertained at a private family of the first respectability in the country.

J H Leigh Hunt *Readings for Railways*

Dialogue I once overheard in a restaurant in London:

Loud customer: I'll see the cart, now.
Waiter: Sorry, sir?
Loud customer: Will you bring me the cart?
Waiter: I'm sorry, sir, I don't know what you mean.
Loud customer: The cart dez vyn.
Waiter: Ah, of course, sir. I'll bring the . . . I'll bring it straight away.

Have you ever tried sake? A small amount served tepid in one of those small china handleless cups is rather good.

Tell Me Not in Figures Wavy

Tell me not in figures wavy
   That my bill is twelve-and-nine.
When I had but soup of gravy
   Steak, potatoes, cheese, and wine.

I'm a poet, I'm a rhymer,
   Hardly versed in trader's tricks,
But a pint of *Laubenheimer*
   Ought not to be four-and-six.

Though I'm not at all unwilling
   To assist you to success,
I must say I think a shilling
   Far too much for watercress.

Bills are long, and cash is fleeting,
   And I wish to make it clear
That the bill you are receipting
   Is the last I settle here.

When you've fleeced your guests and fined them
   I may venture to explain,
They will shake the dust behind them,
   And they won't come back again.

So I leave you, poorer, sadder,
   Lest you make me poorer still:
Sharper than the biting adder
   Is the adder of the bill.

Adrian Ross, quoted in Frank Muir *The Frank Muir Book,* 1976

I think the recent recession has put paid to the most blatant overcharging. In the late eighties I went to a grand London hotel and was charged £4.50 for a glass of still mineral water. I said to the barman, 'I'll give you £2.50, since by my calculation that gives the hotel fair profit on the whole bottle, let alone the single glass I've drunk.'

I'm beginning to sound like Michael Winner.

from The Gourmand

He did not wear his swallow tail,
  But a simple dinner coat;
For once his spirits seemed to fail,
  And his fund of anecdote.
His brow was drawn and damp and pale,
  And a lump stood in his throat.

I never saw a person stare,
  With looks so dour and blue,
Upon the square of bill of fare
  We waiters call the 'M'noo',
And at every dainty mentioned there,
  From *entrée* to *ragoût*.

With head bent low and cheeks aglow,
    He viewed the groaning board,
For he wondered if the chef would show
    The treasures of his hoard,
When a voice behind him whispered low,
    'Sherry or 'ock, m'lord?'

Gods! What a tumult rent the air,
    As with a frightful oath,
He seized the waiter by the hair,
    And cursed him for his sloth;
Then, grumbling like some stricken bear
    Angrily answered, 'Both!'

For each man drinks the thing he loves,
    As tonic, dram, or drug;
Some do it standing, in their gloves,
    Some seated, from a jug;
The upper class from thin-stemmed glass,
    The masses from a mug.

★

Some gorge forsooth in early youth,
    Some wait till they are old;
Some take their fare off earthenware,
    And some from polished gold.
The gourmand gnaws in haste because
    The plates so soon grow cold.

Some eat too swiftly, some too long,
    In restaurant or grill;
Some, when their weak insides go wrong,
    Try a post-prandial pill,
For each man eats his fav'rite meats,
    Yet each man is not ill.

He does not sicken in his bed,
    Through a night of wild unrest,
With a snow-white bandage round his head,
    And a poultice on his breast,
'Neath the nightmare weight of the things he ate
    And omitted to digest.

I know not whether meals be short
   Or whether meals be long;
All that I know of this resort,
   Proves that there's something wrong,
And the soup is weak and tastes of port,
   And the fish is far too strong.

The bread they bake is quite opaque,
   The butter full of hair;
Defunct sardines and flaccid 'greens'
   Are all they give us there.
Such cooking has been known to make
   A common person swear.
           ★

To dance to flutes, to dance to lutes,
   Is a pastime rare and grand;
But to eat of fish, or fowl, or fruits
   To a Blue Hungarian Band
Is a thing that suits nor men nor brutes,
   As the world should understand.
           ★

Six times a table here he booked,
   Six times he sat and scanned
The list of dishes badly cooked
   By the chef's unskilful hand;
And I never saw a man who looked
   So wistfully at the band.

He did not swear or tear his hair,
    But drank up wine galore,
As though it were some vintage rare
    From an old Falernian store;
With open mouth he slaked his drouth,
    And loudly called for more.

He was the type that waiters know,
    Who simply lives to feed,
Who little cares what food we show
    If it be food indeed,
And, when his appetite is low,
    Falls back upon his greed.

For each man eats his fav'rite meats,
    (Provided by his wife);
Or cheese or chalk, or peas or pork,
    (For such, alas! is life!).
The rich man eats them with a fork,
    The poor man with a knife.

Harry Graham (1874–1936)

What a wonderful parody of Oscar Wilde's *Ballad of Reading Gaol*. Mr Graham has hit on an important point: if the food or company are poor, drink as much as you can.

I find life always looks rosier with a bottle of 1988 Clos de Vouveôt, a deliciously round and rich Burgundy with a robust flavour. You will not then be wasting your time.

Why Two Stand Up Together While Drinking the Grace or Loving Cup

The story of the assassination of King Edward is sometimes quoted in illustration of a practice which existed among the Anglo-Saxons. Our forefathers were great drinkers, and it was customary with them, in drinking parties, to pass round a large cup, from which each in turn drank to some of the company. He who thus drank stood up, and as he lifted the cup with both hands, his body was exposed without any defence to a blow, and the occasion was often seized by an enemy to murder him. To prevent this, the following plan was adopted: − When one of the company stood up to drink, he required the companion who sat next to him, or some one of the party, to be his pledge, that is, to be responsible for protecting him against anybody who should attempt to take advantage of his defenceless position; and his companion, if he consented, stood up also, and raised his drawn sword in his hand to defend him while drinking. This practice, in an altered form, continued long after the condition of society had ceased to require it, and was the origin of the modern practice of pledging in drinking. At great festivals, in some of our college halls and city companies, the custom is preserved almost in its primitive form in passing round the ceremonial cup − the loving cup, as it is sometimes called. As each person rises, and takes the cup in his hand to drink, the man seated next to him rises also, and when the latter takes the cup in his turn, the individual next to him does the same.

Charles Tovey *Wit, Wisdom and Morals: Distilled from Bacchus*, 1878

This is probably one of the earliest examples of the Mexican wave. It needs a Mexican wine, but as I have yet to sample the delights of Mexican viniculture and as one of the important tenets is to keep experimenting, I will continue my search. In the meantime let's stray a little from the beaten track and try something new, or rather old, because Spanish conquistadores brought wine into Mexico early in the sixteenth century. They also produced the first wines to be cultivated in North America. So how about a San Lorenzo from Casa Madero (established 1626)?

Sir Robert Viner, Lord Mayor of London, entertained Charles II at a Guildhall banquet and became a little carried away with toasts to the royal family.

The King understood very well how to extricate himself in all kinds of difficulties; and, with a hint to the company to avoid ceremony, stole off, and made towards his coach, which stood ready for him in Guildhall Yard. But the mayor liked his company so well, and was grown so intimate, that he pursued him hastily, and catching him by the hand, cried out with a vehement voice and accent, 'Sir, you shall stay and take t'other bottle!' The airy monarch looked kindly at him over his shoulder, and with a smile and graceful air (for I saw him at the time) repeated this line of the old song –

'He that is drunk is as great as a king,'

and immediately returned back and complied with his landlord.

Spectator No 462

From my experience the line quoted by Charles II rather diminishes royalty. I've found drunks rather boring. But then as people are apt to say, when speaking of royalty, it's a pretty thankless task and one we are all too grateful to be spared.

I think a Château Cheval-Blanc, a classic Graves, displays some of the same fruitiness as the Merry Monarch.

175

Frederic Reynolds, son of the dramatist of the same name, held a dinner party in a cottage he rented one autumn in Highgate and invited a number of friends, among them the poet Samuel Taylor Coleridge. The cottage was small and so, it turned out, were the glasses provided by the host, which led to an original form of after-dinner entertainment.

Our host had replenished his sideboard with fine wines from his father's cellars and wine merchants in town; but having, unluckily, forgotten port, a few bottles of black-strap had been obtained for the nonce from the adjacent inn at Highgate; and sooth to say it was not of the first quality. To add to this grievance, the glasses appertaining to the lodgings were of a diminutive capacity, and when they came to be addressed to champagne and hock, were only tolerable and not to be endured. Thus, in the midst of dinner, or rather more towards the close, we were surprised by Hook's rising, and asking us to fill our bumpers to a toast. It was not difficult to fill these glasses, and we were pledged to follow the example of our leader in draining them. In a brief but most entertaining address he described the excellent qualities of Reynolds, and above all his noble capacity for giving rural dinners, but – there was always a but, not a butt of wine, but a but, a something *manqué*. On this occasion it was but too notorious in the size of those miserable pigmies, out of which we were trying to drink his health etc. etc. etc. The toast was drunk with acclamation, and then followed the exemplary cannikin clink, hob-nobbing, and striking the poor little glasses on the table till every one was broken save one, and that was reserved for a poetical fate.

Tumblers were substituted, and might possibly contribute their share to the early hilarity and consecutive frolic of the night; for ere long Coleridge's sonorous voice was heard declaiming on the extraordinary ebullitions of Hook – 'I have before in the course of my time met with men of admirable promptitude of intellectual power and play of wit, which, as Stillingfleet tells,.

The rays of wit gild whereso'er they strike;

but I never could have conceived such amazing readiness of mind, and resources of genius to be poured out on the mere subject and impulse of the moment.' Having got the poet into this exalted mood, the last of the limited wine-glasses was mounted upon the bottom of a reversed tumbler, and, to the infinite risk of the latter, he was induced to shy at the former with a silver fork, till after two or three throws he succeeded in smashing it into fragments, to be tossed into the basket with its perished brethren. . . . The exhibition was remembered for years afterwards by all who partook of it; and I have a letter of Lockhart's alluding to the date of our witnessing the roseate face of Coleridge, lit up with animation, his large grey eye beaming, his white hair floating, and his whole frame, as it were, radiating with intense interest, as he poised the fork in his hand, and launched it at the fragile object (the last glass of dinner) distant some three or four feet from him on the table!

William Jerdan *Autobiography*, 1852

For part of my childhood I lived opposite the graveyard where Coleridge is buried. This is not the famous Highgate Cemetery but a smaller one next to a church in the centre of the village. In the famous cemetery there used to be a wonderful old man who showed people around. Having led tired, usually damp groups around various tombs, he reached the climax of his tour – Karl Marx's tomb. Next to Marx is the tomb of a lesser known individual, a Mr Spencer. At this point the old man would remark, 'There you are, what all the tourists come for – Marks and Spencer!'

If you're going to break the glasses there's no point in spending a fortune on the wine, so here are two cheap and cheerful suggestions: the red is a 1992 Cabernet Sauvignon Special Reserve, Vanel and a suitable white would be a Saget Blanc from the Sancerre region.

In vino veritas is an old saying, but scarcely a true one. Men's minds, when elevated by wine, or anything else, become apt to exaggeration of feeling of every kind. I have often found *In vino asperitas* to be a much truer *dictum*.

Sir Morgan O'Doherty, Bart *Maxims*

How true! Alas how true!

The only answer is a soothing dessert wine to sweeten sharp tempers and sharp words and I can think of nothing better than one from the Willi Opitz Winery, situated south-east of Vienna. The vineyards have been in the Opitz family for many generations. In 1975, when Willi took control, the serious wine-making began. In 1988 he produced twenty-seven different wines from his two hectares of vines. If your bank balance can stand it, I suggest you treat yourself, and any warring factions, to a half-bottle of Welschriesling Eiswen, guaranteed to restore sweetness and light after the unfortunate utterance of a few best-forgotten home truths.

In the time of Henry VIII wine was used at breakfast with beer; and even the grave Sir Thomas More drank frequent bumpers in the morning before proceeding to state business. Of this learned statesman is recorded the following anecdote:

Sir Thomas More was sent by Henry VIII as ambassador to a foreign court. The morning he was to have his audience, knowing the virtue of wine, he ordered his servant to bring him a large glass of Sack, and having drank that he called for another. The servant, with officious ignorance, would have dissuaded him from a second draught, but in vain. The ambassador drank off a second, and demanded a third, which he also drained, insisting on a fourth; he was persuaded by his servant to let it alone. He then went to his audience. When, however, he returned home, he called for his servant, and threatened him with his cane. 'You rogue,' said he, 'what have you done me? I spoke so to the Emperor, on the inspiration of those three first glasses that I drank, that he told me I was fit to govern three parts of the world. Now, you dog! If I had drunk the fourth glass, I had been fit to govern all the world.'

Charles Tovey *Wit, Wisdom and Morals: Distilled from Bacchus*, 1878

One leader who drank copious amounts was Winston Churchill, whose consumption of brandy and champagne was astonishing. His favourite champagne was Pol Roger and for twenty-five years there was a black band round the outside of the label in mourning of his death. Pol Roger is available as a non-vintage, but if you really want to toast our great wartime leader in the style in which he was accustomed, see if you can find this wine with good bottle age. If you do, I want to know, and quickly, where you bought it and how much it cost.

On the drinking habits of the Elizabethan Irish rebel Shane O'Neil . . .

Subtle and crafty he was, especially in the morning, and much given to excessive gulping and surfeiting. And, albeit, he had most commonly two hundred tuns of wines in his cellar at Dundrum, and had his fill thereof, yet was he never satisfied till he had swallowed up marvellous great quantities of usquebaugh, or *aqua vitæ,* of that country, whereof so immeasurably he would drink and have, that for the quenching of the heat of his body, which by that means was extremely inflamed and distempered, he was ofttimes conveyed (as the common report was) into a deep pit, and, standing upright in the same, the earth was cast round about him up to the hard chin, and there he did remain until such time as his body recovered to some temperature.

Raphael Holinshed *The Chronicles of England, Scotland and Ireland,*
1577, 1587

Nowadays, of course, he'd have a swimming-pool. But I am something of a traditionalist and am constantly asking my wife to dig large holes in the back lawn!

Now this little gem is a salutary reminder that Irish whiskey, the *aqua vitæ* referred to, is absolutely delightful and slips down remarkably easily. One of the best of the modern Irish whiskies in my opinion is Jameson's and fortunately the Irish have generously chosen to share it with the rest of the world.

On the drinking habits of 'the best society' around 1815 . . .

Drinking and play were more universally indulged in then than at
the present time, and many men still living must remember the
couple of bottles of port, at least, which accompanied his dinner in
those days. Indeed, female society, amongst the upper classes, was
most notoriously neglected; except, perhaps by romantic foreigners,
who were the heroes of many a fashionable adventure that fed the
clubs with ever acceptable scandal. How could it be otherwise,
when husbands spent their days in the hunting-field, or were
entirely occupied with politics, and always away from home during
the day; whilst the dinner party, commencing at seven or eight,
frequently did not break up before one in the morning. There

were then four and even five bottle men; and the only thing that saved them was drinking very slowly, and out of very small glasses. The learned head of the law, Lord Eldon, and his brother, Lord Stowell, used to say that they had drunk more bad port than any two men in England; indeed, the former was rather apt to be overtaken, and to speak occasionally somewhat thicker than natural after long and heavy potations. The late Lords Panmure, Dufferin, and Blayney, wonderful to relate, were six bottle men at this time; and I really think that if 'the good society of 1815' could appear before their more moderate descendants, in the state they were generally reduced to after dinner, the moderns would pronounce their ancestors fit for nothing but bed.

Captain Rees Howell Gronow *Reminiscences,* 1888

One hundred and eighty years on I doubt if 'the good society of 1815' would survive modern press scrutiny. Poor Lord George-Brown would have been rated a novice alongside these grand topers and we all remember what happened when the press spotted him having a bit of trouble in a gutter.

As I've mentioned earlier the port I occasionally sip is Warre's '75. However, if you want to go for something even older without completely breaking the bank, go for Quinta do Noval Nacional. The label will certainly impress your guests if you mix in impressionable circles.

Twistleton Fiennes, the late Lord Saye and Sele . . . was a very eccentric man, and the greatest epicure of his day. His dinners were worthy of the days of Vitellius or Heliogabalus. Every country, every sea, was searched and ransacked to find some new delicacy for our British Sybarite. I remember, at one of his breakfasts, an omelette being served which was composed entirely of golden pheasants' eggs. He had a very strong constitution, and would drink absinth and curaçao in quantities which were perfectly awful to behold. These stimulants produced no effect upon his brain; but his health gradually gave way under the excesses of all kinds in which he indulged. He was a kind, liberal, and good natured man, but a very odd fellow. I shall never forget the astonishment of a servant I had recommended to him. On entering his service, John made his appearance as Fiennes was going out to dinner, and asked his new master if he had any orders. He received the following answer – 'Place two bottles of sherry by my bedside, and call me the day after tomorrow.'

Captain Rees Howell Gronow *Reminiscences,* 1888

To drink absinthe and curaçao 'in quantities which were perfectly awful to behold' proves that one thing is certain, the noble lord did not treat his body like a temple. For myself I've always viewed alcohol at breakfast the beginning of a dangerously slippery slope. I have my own golden rule which is that I never touch *any* alcohol, not even sherry trifle at lunch time, until I've finished work. This means that if I'm working in the theatre I don't have any alcohol until about eleven o'clock at night. After which, dear reader, I do my very best to make up for lost time. By that stage certain things, red wine for example, no longer appeal. As an alternative to white wine, a weak brandy, ice and soda is just the thing. Any run-of-the-mill cognac will do. Save the vintage Armagnac for after dinner in the company of good friends.

The unfortunate Mr Green was less familiar with student beverages than his undergraduate colleagues – as experience showed:

And when he had hastily tossed off another glass of milk-punch (merely to clear his throat), he felt bold enough to answer the spirit-rappings which were again demanding 'Mr Green's song!' It was given much in the following manner:

Mr Verdant Green (in low, plaintive tones, and fresh alarm at hearing the sounds of his own voice). 'I dreamt that I dwe-elt in mar-arble halls, with' –

Mr Bouncer (interrupting). 'Spit it out, Gig-lamps! Dis child can't hear whether it's Maudlin Hall you're singing about, or what.'

Omnes. 'Order! or-*der!* Shut up, Bouncer!'

Charles Larkyns (encouragingly). 'Try back, Verdant: never mind.'

Mr Verdant Green (tries back, with increased confusion of ideas, resulting principally from the milk-punch and tobacco). 'I dreamt that I dwe-elt in mar-arble halls, with vassals and serfs at my si-hi-hide; and – and – I beg your pardon, gentlemen, I really forgot – oh, I know! – and I also dre-eamt, which ple-eased me most – no, that's not it' –

Mr Bouncer (who does not particularly care for the words of a song, but only appreciates the chorus) − 'That'll do, old feller! We ain't pertickler, − *(rushes with great deliberation and noise to the chorus)* 'That you lo-oved me sti-ill the sa-ha-hame − chorus, gentlemen!'

Omnes (in various keys and time). 'That you lo-oved me sti-ill the same.'

Mr Bouncer (to Mr Green, alluding remotely to the opera). 'Now my Bohemian gal, can't you come out tonight? Spit us out a yard or two more, Gig-lamps.'

Mr Verdant Green (who has again taken the opportunity to clear his throat). 'I dreamt that I dwe-elt in mar-arble − no! I beg pardon! sang the *(desperately)* − that sui-uitors sou-ought my hand, that knights on their *(hic)* ben-ended kne-e-ee − had *(hic)* riches too gre-eat to! −' *(Mr Verdant Green smiles benignantly upon the company)* − Don't rec'lect anymo.

Mr Bouncer (who is not to be defrauded of the chorus). 'Chorus, gentlemen! − That you'll lo-ove me sti-ill the sa-a-hame!'

Omnes (ad libitum). 'That you'll lo-ove me sti-ill the same!' . . .

When the chorus had been sung over three or four times, and Mr Verdant Green's name had been proclaimed with equal noise, that gentleman rose (with great difficulty), to return thanks. He was understood to speak as follows :−

'Genelum anladies *(cheers)*, − I meaangenelum. *('That's about the ticket, old feller!' from Mr Bouncer.)* Customd syam plic speakn, I − I − *(hear, hear)* − feel bliged drinkmyel. I'm fresman, genelum, and prow title *(loud cheers)*. Myfren Misserboucer, fallowme callm myfren! *('In course, Gig-lamps, you do me proud, old feller.')* Myfren Misserboucer seszime fresman − prow title, sure you *(hear, hear)*. Genelmun, werall jolgoodfles, anwe wogohotill-morrin! *('We won't, we won't not a bit of it!')* Gelmul, I'm freshmal, an namesgreel, gelmul *(cheers)*. Fanyul dousmewor, herescardinpock 'Iltellm! Misser Verdalgreel, Braseface, Oxul fresmal, anprowtitle *(Great cheering and rattling of glasses, during which Mr Verdant Green's coat-tails are made the receptacles for empty bottles, lobsters' claws, and other miscellaneous articles.)* Misserboucer said was fresmal. If Misserboucer wantsultme *('No, no!')*, herescardinpocklltellmenamesverdalgreel, Braseface! Not shameofitgelmul! prowttitle! *(Great applause.)* I doewaltilsul

Misserboucer! thenwhysee sultme? theaswas Iwaltknow! *(Loud cheers, and roars of laughter, in which Mr Verdant Green suddenly joins to the best of his ability.)* I'm anoxful fresmal, gelmul, 'fmyfrel Misserboucer loumecallimso. *(Cheers and laughter, in which Mr Verdant Green feebly joins.)* Anwer all jolgoodfles, anwe wogohotilmorril, an I'm fresmal, gelmul, anfanyul dowsmewor – and I – doefeel quiwell!'

This was the termination of Mr Verdant Green's speech, for after making a few unintelligible sounds, his knees suddenly gave way, and with a benevolent smile he disappeared beneath the table.

Cuthbert Bede (Edward Bradley) *The Adventures of Mr Verdant Green,*
1853-7

When I was a young man at Nottingham Repertory Theatre two actors decided before a matinée to play a game called drinking the flags. The basis for this is very simple. If you're drinking the Union Jack, you have a measure of gin, some red wine and some blue curaçao. This pair had reached Greece, via Austria, Belgium, Canada, Denmark, Ethiopia (particularly dangerous) and France before they were stopped by the theatre barman.

Neither of the actors was due to appear until the opening of the second act. The curtain went up with the actors facing each other from separate sides of the stage. They were playing French army officers in charge of training conscripts. This involved barking orders at young actors grouped upstage. Actor One made a vague attempt at speech which came out as incomprehensible gurgles and belches before he made a rapid exit into the wings to be sick. Actor Two started a high-pitched and hysterical giggling before sinking to the floor. Whereupon the situation was saved by the remarkable leading man who walked onto the stage ahead of cue, did all the lines of the two 'absent' actors, arranged for the conscripts to carry off the second of them and proceeded to manage all the parts himself. I hope I'm never required to show similar heroism.

My advice is *never* try and drink the flags. If you must,

then stay away from flags containing blue, green, yellow and orange. If you must drink before the show, you could do worse than follow Noël Coward's dictum for first nights: everybody associated with the show should have half a glass of champagne to take the edge off their nerves. Perhaps Coward, as star, author and director, allowed himself three half-glasses. Perrier-Jouet has a suitably theatrical bottle and is very reliable.

A Restoration rake on drinking . . .

To unbosom myself frankly and freely to your Grace, I always looked upon drunkenness to be an unpardonable crime in a young fellow, who without any of these foreign helps, has fire enough in his veins to enable him to do justice to Caelia whenever she demands a tribute from him. In a middle-aged man, I consider the bottle only as subservient to the nobler pleasures of love; and he that would suffer himself to be so far infatuated by it as to neglect the pursuit of a more agreeable game I think deserves no quarter from the ladies: In old age, indeed, when tis convenient very often to forget and steal from ourselves, I am of opinion that a little drunkenness, discreetly used, may as well contribute to our health of body as tranquillity of soul.

I am, my Lord, your Grace's most obedient servant

Sir George Etherege (?1634-91)

How comforting that alcohol consumption can increase to make up for loss of sexual prowess. Macbeth's porter discovered that too much drink can provoke the desire but take away the performance, though that need not always be the case. I prefer to think that in the right circumstances, the right wine can have the right effect. To that end here's an engaging little joke.

Donald Duck is making one of his many films in Hollywood. One Friday lunchtime the director says to him, 'Donald, you've been great this week and we're so far ahead of schedule that I'm giving everyone the rest of the day off. You don't have to be back until Monday.'

'Thanks a million,' says Donald. So he walks towards his dressing-room and on the way he sees the most beautiful girl duck he's ever set eyes on.

She sees Donald and immediately goes over to him. 'Mr Duck, Mr Duck,' she begins.

'Donald . . . please. Call me Donald.'

'OK,' she replies, shyly.

'What's your name?'

'Rose.'

'Gee, that's a beautiful name. Have you finished for the day?' asked Donald.

'Finished, period. It was only a small part in a Mr Magoo film. Can I have your autograph, Donald?'

'Why, sure. Come to my dressing-room and I'll sign a photo for you.'

As they walk back to Donald's dressing-room he says, 'Know where I'm going for the weekend?'

'No,' says Rose.

'Well, there's this great hotel about seventy-five miles away from here, right on the coast. From one side you face the sea, from the other side you face the mountains. It's a great place. Good air and good food.'

'It sounds absolutely wonderful,' says Rose.

Donald asks, 'Well . . . do you want to come with me. No funny business. Separate rooms, if that's what you want.'

Rose looks blissfully happy and says, 'One room, Donald, overlooking the ocean.'

So they arrive at the hotel and have a wonderful evening, sitting on the balcony of their suite, watching the sun set, sipping champagne and eating the most delicious room-service dinner.

At the end of the evening they climb into bed together and very tenderly embrace.

Then Rose says, 'Donald, do you have any condoms?'

Donald says, 'No, but I'll go down to the concierge. He'll have some.'

So, Donald puts on his dressing-gown and goes down to the concierge and asks for a packet of condoms.

The concierge says, 'Certainly, sir,' and hands the pack over.

Just as Donald turns away, the concierge enquires, 'Shall I put them on your bill, sir?'

Donald says, 'What sort of pervert do you think I am?'

To return to Etherege, the Restoration led to a revival of interest in all things French. A classic wine which I would certainly regard as compensation for practically anything is Château Mouton-Rothschild. Any vintage is rewarding, but if you can get hold of the '61 you will embrace old age with as much satisfaction as anything livelier.

The Tale of Lord Lovell

Lord Lovell, he stood at his own front door,
    Seeking the hole for the key;
His hat was wrecked, and his trousers bore
    A rent across either knee,
When down came the beauteous Lady Jane
    In fair white draperie.

'Oh, where have you been, Lord Lovell?' she said,
    'Oh, where have you been?' said she;
'I have not closed an eye in bed,
    And the clock has just struck three.
Who has been standing you on your head
    In the ash-barrel, pardie?'

'I am not drunk, Lad' Shane,' he said:
    'And so late it cannot be;
The clock struck one as I enterèd –
    I heard it two times or three;
It must be the salmon on which I fed
    Has been too many for me.'

'Go tell your tale, Lord Lovell,' she said,
    'To the maritime cavalree,
To your grandmother of the hoary head –
    To any one but me:
The door is not used to be openèd
    With a cigarette for a key.'

Anonymous

I chose this piece because I found it an hilarious parody of the tedious old English and Scots ballads I endured as a schoolboy. I particularly enjoy the oblique reference to 'Go tell it to the marines!'

A bit of advice when returning to your partner in a state

of advanced drunkenness: don't make excuses and above all don't try and act sober, it compounds the felony. I used to be rather good at acting sober when drunk; no slurring of speech, no swaying. But after about ten minutes I always wanted to visit the bathroom and every time I attempted this I ended up with a loud crash in the broom cupboard opposite the bathroom door and blew my cover completely.

The best thing is to stay sober. Never mix spirits with wine (and that includes cognac). Buy a wine you really like, not necessarily an expensive wine, but one which you sip for enjoyment rather than tip down for its alcohol alone. A wine I always enjoy and can thoroughly recommend is a Tokay Pinot-Gris from Alsace. This white is perfect as an aperitif, with food and to take you through the evening.

Grattan recalls the one occasion on which Edmund Kean's enthusiasm for the bottle prevented the great actor from appearing on the London stage.

He had never, I believe, yet disappointed a London audience, but on one occasion. The circumstances of this one he often related to me. He had gone to dine somewhere about ten miles from town with some old friends of early days, players, of course, fully intending to be at the theatre in time for the evening's performance. But temptation and the bottle were too strong for him. He out-stayed his time, got drunk, and lost all recollection of Shakespeare, Shylock, Drury Lane, and the duties they entailed on him. His friends, frightened at the indiscretion they had caused, dispatched Kean's servant, with his empty chariot, and a well-framed story that the horses had been frightened, near the village where Kean had dined, at a flock of geese by the roadside; that the carriage was upset, and the unfortunate tragedian's shoulder dislocated. This story was repeated from the stage by the manager; and the rising indignation of the audience (who had suffered the entertainments to be commenced by the farce) was instantly calmed down into commiseration and regret.

The following morning Kean was shocked and bewildered at discovering the truth of his situation. But how must his embarrassment have been increased on learning, that several gentlemen had already arrived from town to make inquiries for him? He jumped out of bed; and, to his infinite affright, he saw, amongst the carriages, those of Sir Francis Burdett, Mr Whitbread, and others of his leading friends, whose regard for him brought them to see into his situation in person.

Luckily for him, his old associates the actors had, with great presence of mind, carried on the deception of the preceding night. The village apothecary lent himself to it and with a grave countenance confirmed the report; and Kean himself was obliged to become a party, *nolens volens,* in the hoax. His chamber was accordingly darkened, his face whitened, his arm bandaged. A few of the most distinguished inquirers were admitted to his bed-side. No one discovered the cheat; and, to crown it completely, he appeared, in an incredibly short time, on the boards of old Drury again, the public being carefully informed that his respect and gratitude towards them urged him to risk the exertion, notwithstanding his imperfect convalescence, and to go through the arduous parts of Richard, Macbeth, and Othello, on three successive nights, with his arm in a sling!

Thomas Grattan *Beaten Paths,* 1862

The stories of actors being drunk are legion. The saddest one to my mind is that of the late, great Cyril Cusack. As a young man he was playing in *The Doctor's Dilemma.* On St Patrick's Day he got so drunk that he was unable to perform. His understudy didn't know the lines and the performance had to be cancelled. I cannot be sure, but I think the impresario was Binkie Beaumont, one of the most powerful men in the British theatre. The next day he said to the young Cusack, 'You will never work in the West End again', and to my knowledge, except for an appearance representing Ireland in one of Peter Daubeny's World Theatre Seasons, he did not appear in the West End again until the end of his career. This petty act deprived London theatre-goers of one of the finest actors of the century.

A wine which would have consoled both Kean and Cusack is the exquisite Château Fuissé Vieilles Vignes, one of the best white wines I've ever tasted.

Song of the Decanter

There was an old decanter, and
its mouth was gaping wide; the
rosy wine had ebbed away
and left its crystal
side; and the
wind went
humming –
humming up
and down: the
wind it blew, and
through the
reed-like
hollow neck
the wildest notes it
blew. I placed it in the
window, where the blast was
blowing free, and fancied that its pale
mouth sang the queerest strains to me.
'They tell me – puny conquerors! the Plague
has slain his ten, and war his hundred thousand of
the very best of men; but I' – 'twas thus the Bottle
spoke – 'but I have conquered more than all your
famous conquerors, so feared and famed of yore.
Then come, ye youths and maidens all, come
drink from out my cup, the beverage that dulls
the brain and burns the spirits up; that puts to
shame your conquerors that slay their scores
below; for this has deluged millions with the
lava tide of woe. Tho' in the path of battle
darkest streams of blood may roll; yet while
I killed the body, I have damn'd the very
soul. The cholera, the plague, the sword,
such ruin never wrought, as I in mirth or
malice on the innocent have brought.
And still I breathe upon them, and
they shrink before my breath, and year
by year my thousands tread   the
dusty   way   of   death.'

Anonymous (from Carolyn Wells's *Whimsy Anthology*), 1906

I'm convinced chianti has declined in popularity since they stopped putting it in those lovely raffia-covered bottles. Some people are suspicious of unusual bottles. I'm not one of them as I mentioned in the introduction. I'm an admirer of the Willi Opitz wine all of which come in distinctive long, narrow, thin-necked bottles.

One wine which I think works well decanted, to accompany this piece, is Château Respide Medeville from Graves: '86 was a particularly good year.

Drinking Song

There are people, I know, to be found,
  Who say, and apparently think,
That sorrow and care may be drowned
  By a timely consumption of drink.

Does not man, these enthusiasts ask,
  Most nearly approach the divine,
When engaged in the soul-stirring task
  Of filling his body with wine?

Have not beggars been frequently known,
  When satisfied, soaked and replete,
To imagine their bench was a throne
  And the civilized world at their feet?

Lord Byron has finely described
  The remarkably soothing effect
Of liquor, profusely imbibed,
  On a soul that is shattered and wrecked.

In short, if your body or mind
  Or your soul or your purse come to grief,
You need only get drunk, and you'll find
  Complete and immediate relief.

For myself, I have managed to do
  Without having recourse to this plan,
So I can't write a poem for you,
  And you'd better get someone who can.

J K Stephen, 1898

Obviously a teetotaller – but at least a witty one. Sadly, in my view, no one has yet satisfactorily conquered the problem of making a truly successful non-alcoholic wine. A good old-fashioned ginger beer is my recommendation for our teetotal friends.

To Make Wine Settle Well

Take a pint of wheat and boil it in a quart of water, till it burst and become soft; then squeeze it through a linen cloth, and put a pint of liquor into the hogshead of unsettled white wine; stir it well about and it will become fine.

To Detect Adulterated Wine

Heat equal parts of oyster-shells and sulphur together, and keep them in a white heat for fifteen minutes, and when cold, mix them with an equal quantity of cream of tartar; put this mixture into a strong bottle with common water to boil for one hour, and then decant into ounce phials, and add 20 drops of muriatic acid to each; this liquor precipitates the least quantity of lead, copper, &c. from wines in a very sensible black precipitate.

To Render Red Wine White

If a few quarts of well-skimmed milk be put to a hogshead of red wine, it will soon precipitate the greater part of the colour, and leave the whole nearly white; and this is of known use in the turning of red wines, when pricked, into white; in which a small degree of acidity is not so much perceived.

Milk is, from this quality of discharging colour from wines, of use also to the wine-coopers, for the whitening of wines that have acquired a brown colour from the cask, or from having been hastily boiled before fermenting; for the addition of a little skimmed milk, in these cases, precipitates the brown colour, and leaves wines of almost limpid, or of what they call a water whiteness, which is much coveted abroad in wines as well as brandies.

Samuel and Sarah Adams *The Complete Servant*, 1825

The first two sections are delightful, all the more so because of the ready accessibility through your favourite local supermarket, of oyster-shells, pints of wheat and muriatic acid!

The last section on rendering red wine white might throw

an entirely different light on our Lord's first and most famous miracle. Was he turning water into wine, or was it actually milk?

As an interesting half-way house between white and red you might like to try one of the new golden-pinky Tokays made, perversely, in the old-fashioned way. It's a very interesting taste and quite different from what you'd expect from Tokay.

With decanters – those half-way houses between bottle and glass – one comes to questions of pure art. They can be very lovely things indeed; they can be frightfully ugly; and it is possible to have them without any great outlay – or was possible when it was possible to have anything without a great outlay – good to look at and good to use. Body-colour, when they are not kept pure white, should be, I think, restricted to a pale green – the shade of a moselle flask. Blues and reds kill the natural hues of wine, though a not too deep yellow is permissible. The noblest decanter I ever possessed was one I saw stuck away on a high shelf at Powells' (whose departure, by the way, from Whitefriars is sad). It had been made to order for the contents of a 'tappit-hen' (*v. sup.*), but rejected by the (saving his reverence) idiotic orderer, and I bought it. It was of the flattened cone shape, white, fluted, and with a little frill round its fair throat. Unfortunately I never could get an actual tappit hen of claret to put in – they were not infrequent at the sale of old Scotch cellars thirty or forty years ago, but are very rare now. However, it contented itself with a magnum cheerfully enough: and I am not sure that the bouquet did not develop better for the empty space. (I need hardly say that to decant more than one bottle into the same vessel is a very risky experiment.) At any rate it used to look imposing under a seven-light brass candlestick which Mr Benson made for me. The same admirable craftsmen, who, like all persons deserving that noun and adjective, would take just as much trouble for you if you gave them a half-guinea order as if it had been such as one of their commissions I once saw on its way to Russia – a cut-glass service worth fifteen hundred pounds – made me a set of claret jugs, two of each size – pint, bottle, and magnum – of the pilgrim bottle shape, green, fluted, but with rounded bottoms, not flat like the 'hen-master'. And from them, from Salviati's, and from other sources one picked up things not unworthy of their intended contents.

The one drawback of cut-glass decanters – besides their cost, but apart from the purpose recommended by Count Considine in *Charles O'Malley* – is their great weight. The beauty of them no one can well contest; though I think the material shews better in the wine-glass than in the decanter. Few kinds shew off the wine itself better than the so-called 'Black Forest' type, which separates a top and a bottom mass of liquid by four slender tube-columns. My earliest recollection of it (I do not think it was at all common before the middle of the nineteenth century) was derived from mounted examples in the window of a silversmith named Sachs, who used to have a shop – the only one in a highly genteel neighbourhood – below Connaught Square, and close to that quaint chapel and burying-ground which, according to legend, saw the 'resurrecting' of Sterne's body. This was as far back as the early fifties. Afterwards they multiplied, and were even sold with whisky and other things in them, so that they have become quite common.

But that matters little. Of more elaborate forms, curly snaky things, circlets with a big hole in the middle and the like, I am not sure. Simplicity is a mighty Goddess in the flagon, which should aim at displaying not so much itself as the wine.

George Saintsbury *Notes on a Cellar-Book,* 1920

Like any wine buff, my library has its copy of George Saintsbury's famous work. However, the wine writers for whom I have most regard are Hugh Johnson (particularly his *World Atlas of Wine*), Anthony Hanson, who wrote the definitive book on Burgundy, André Simon and Elizabeth David, my admiration for whom has already been expressed.

Compared with them, Saintsbury comes over as rather old-fashioned. To match this extract I have therefore chosen the type of wine one would offer a favourite godfather, a 1983 Château de la Rivière. This is a conservative choice, a claret from an area that was popular before Saint-Emilion became the best-known of the clarets.

On cleaning decanters . . .

Cut some thick brown paper into very small bits, so as to go with ease into the decanter; shred a little soap very fine, and put it, together with some milk-warm water, into the decanters. The water must on no account be hot, or it will certainly split the glass. If the decanter be very dirty, add a little pearl-ash.

By the end of a piece of cane with a bit of sponge tied at one end, you will, by working this mixture about in the decanter, soon remove the crust or stain of the wine, and, by rinsing the glass once or twice with clean cold water, it will have a very fine polish.

When the decanters have been properly washed, turn them down in a rack to dry, or for want of a rack, into a jug, to drain thoroughly; for if not used for some time, and spots of damp have been left in them, a kind of mildew will be formed, which will injure the flavour of whatever is put therein, and prevent the decanter having that clear bright lustre which all clean glass should always possess.

James Williams *The Footman's Guide*, 1847

To paraphrase Mrs Beeton, 'First find your footman' – mine's been missing for years. But I do think, should you be lucky enough to find one, you should let him see this excellent piece of advice. Since the footman will probably have a better knowledge of your cellar than you do, I suggest you reward him from time to time with a bottle of good, red Burgundy – a 1976 Musigny from Faiveley would fit the bill nicely.

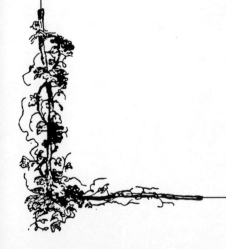

Although I have made remarks in another place on the management of claret in wood and in bottle, I copy here instructions which have been transmitted by a friend in Bordeaux. These apply equally to burgundy, &c.:

The quality of the wine must not be judged on its arrival, because it is affected by the voyage.

If the hogshead is cased, uncase it.

Place the cask in the cellar, so that the bung is on its side and covered by the wine, to prevent the air from penetrating.

Avoid frequent tasting.

After a rest of about a month, draw off the wine into bottles – the latter must be quite clean.

Take great care that the cask is not moved, or the wine will become cloudy, and there will be a deposit in the bottles.

The corks must be new, and of good quality, and firmly driven in.

By attending to the above precautions the wine will never become acid.

Use only the best sealing-wax; the common kind has always an unpleasant smell, which is often communicated to the cork and to the wine.

When the drawing-off is nearly completed, raise the cask very gently, so that what still remains may be rendered as little thick as possible.

Lay aside the last drawn bottles, which are inferior, and from which the quality must not be judged.

The bottles should be laid on their sides in a dry cellar.

Great attention should be paid not to put the wine into bottle until it is in good condition, and the weather is fine and clear.

Although the wine can be drunk immediately after it is bottled, it is only after several months that its quality can be appreciated; more especially the high growths, in which the flavour and bouquet are only gradually developed during several years.

It often happens that a house which has received our wines in cask one year, write for exactly the same the next.

If the wine first sent remains in the cask, there will be no difference between the first and the second. If, on the contrary, the first has been put into bottle, it will be better; Bordeaux wines improving much more in bottle than in cask.

These precautions are necessary in order to drink the wines of Bordeaux with pleasure. Old bottled wines will inevitably form a little deposit, and, if this is mixed with the wine, it detracts considerably from the taste and delicacy of the bouquet. It is therefore indispensable, before tasting the wine, to let it rest for about a month; then, when it is required, uncork without shaking or moving it, and, almost without changing its position, decant it slowly into another bottle, leaving the deposit at the bottom of the first.

This operation, which only occupies a few minutes, is generally practised in Bordeaux, and wherever fine wines are appreciated.

Thomas George Shaw *The Wine, the Vine and the Cellar*, 1863

As I mentioned in the introduction, following a few simple guidelines on how you store wine can make a great difference to its condition when you drink it. Wine should always be stored in a cool temperature away from natural light. If you don't happen to have a cellar, a cupboard under the stairs can be a near perfect storage location.

As for a wine to lay down I would go for a 1993 red Burgundy in particular Latricières-Chambertin from Domaine Rossignol-Trapet.

My cellar near Cambridge had one awkward peculiarity. It was approached through another of slightly lower level, and this outer cellar, at certain times of the year, used to be filled about a foot deep with the most pellucid water, apparently rising from the earth. This remained some time, and disappeared as it came. While it was there it necessitated the erection of a plank bridge to get to the wine, and incidentally made the house above rather damp. So a kind friend proposed to pump it out, and actually brought a garden-engine for the purpose. I had, while expressing due gratitude, to point out to him that in that case we should be pumping against the springs of half Cambridgeshire and an unknown proportion of Essex and Suffolk, so that on the general principle of water finding its level, the operation would take some time, and it might be difficult to know what to do with what we pumped. I believe new waterworks, for Cambridge itself, have since accomplished this piece of engineering more satisfactorily. Had I been longer there the damp would, no doubt, have worked wreckage. The butler at a house in Hampshire, which, though situated high up, must have had springs near it, told me that it was there hardly safe to leave wine, without actual recorking, for more than seven years. But in this instance I had small supplies, and moved in half that time, so no harm was done.

When, in 1895, I moved once more from another place in the south of England to Edinburgh, I inhabited, for the first four years, a large house somewhat to the west of the city, and dating from the early eighteenth century. Cellars of such houses in Scotland are generally ample; I know one in which even Mr Crotchet's 'thousand dozen of wine' could be accommodated with the greatest ease, and leave room for at least another thousand, with casks to match. But though my abode had a large cellarage, it had evidently not – recently at least – been much used for the noblest purpose of such structures. There was an enormous coal-cellar, which one could and of course did – in the good days when colliers, *pace* Mr Smillie, were quite happy with their moderate wages, and when coal merchants charged no more than twelve shillings a ton in summer – fill for a whole year's consumption on the rather extravagant Northern scale. There was an intermediate apartment, hardly at all binned, but where you could put cases, casks, and iron wine bins if you chose. And then there was the innermost recess, which was prepared – after a fashion but not very amply – for wine storage.

It was greatly infested with rats, and for a time I was puzzled by having to add thermometers to the already considerable list of rat-foods. But before very long I found out the mystery. In looking to see that the cellar was not too cold (there was not much danger of its being too hot) one sloped the candle towards the instrument, and the grease dropped on the wood. It hung just above the top of an iron wine bin, and the ingenious beasts evidently climbed up without displacing the bottles. They, to do them justice, never lost me a drop that way, though they seem to have had designs, for we once discovered a sherry glass half-way down a rat hole. But their enemy, my Scotch terrier Bounce (whose pedigree I used to keep in the same drawer with my commission as Regius Professor) was more clumsy. He followed me one day without my knowledge, saw a rat, dashed at the bin, and I immediately found him yelling with fear and struggling with the *débris* and froth of two magnums of champagne. If he had got the rat it would have been some consolation for a rather expensive kind of sport.

George Saintsbury *Notes on a Cellar-Book*, 1920

In comparison with poor Professor Saintsbury's Cambridge home conditions in my cellar seem positively antiseptic. One can only wonder whether Bounce's pedigree encouraged him to lap up some of the '*débris* and froth' – or did the rat claim it as part of its bounty?

And how to replace the professor's two lost magnums? Perhaps I could suggest a couple of magnums of 1981 Réserve de Krug which has benefited from a more extended period of time on the 'lees', giving it even greater depth and complexity, than the already splendid champagnes from the House of Krug. I'm sure Professor Saintsbury would agree.

The nineteenth-century author of this extract, and his two companions, gained entrance, somewhat illicitly, to the London Dock Wine Cellars, entering a subterranean Mecca access to which would have been envied by wine lovers the world over.

An arched stone doorway, opening on a flight of damp and dirty steps leading to dusky subterranean regions, with a glimmer of lamps at the bottom – this was our destination. It was impossible not to feel somewhat nervous as we descended into the weird darkness. We made merry; but I know we all felt somewhat timid. But down we went; and he of us who assumed, in recognition of his former experience, the post of acting manager, waved the tasting order (a talismanic piece of paper, that bears upon it words to the effect that Messrs Port, Negus, and Co. sent greeting to their cooper, in the London Dock Wine Cellars, and desired him to let Mr Smith – we will say, not to be too personal – and party taste the wines thereon mentioned) in a lushy-looking official's face, who forthwith assured himself of the regularity of our passport, and then called the cooper. Up he came out of the dim vaulted passage that stretched away before us; and, furnishing us with a lamp apiece, stuck at the end of a piece of wood resembling a wooden butter-slice, we followed him into the darkness.

As only my very first impressions remain vividly in my mind, I will tell you what they were. In the first place, before I had walked a hundred yards, I had half made up my mind to secrete a gimlet about my person some fine day, and get lost, of maliced prepense, in the vaults. Wine! You have no idea – unless, like me, you have been to the 'docks' – what a quantity there is of it hard away down by the river. I listened to the cooper's account of the extent of the cellars – of thirteen acres of wine here, and ten there – till I well-nigh resolved I would never leave the spot. We walked for minutes along a path walled in by wine – it was before us in an interminable vista of butts and barrels; it stretched in collateral avenues, and ran in right-angled profusion across our path –

Pipes to the right of us – Pipes to the left of us –
Pipes, too, behind us – ripened and crusted!

But, at last, after taking in I don't know how much through the pores, like Joey Ladle, the cooper stopped, and we formed an anxious group round a cask of charming proportions. By a freak of that fancy, which in your correspondent is so constantly at play, I had said to my comrades before coming down, 'Let us assume the names of Brown, Jones, and Robinson. We did so – I was Brown; my tall friend, Jones; my little friend, Robinson. So, looking as much as we could like that eminent firm – we waited, in thirsty suspense, the operations which were to set flowing, for our behoof, the generous stream. The gimlet, after a few energetic twists, pierced the jealous plank that guarded so well the vinous treasures within; it was withdrawn, and a tiny pipe inserted in the hole it had made; then a vigorous suck from the cooper, and there was a grateful gurgle heard, and an amber-coloured liquid came bubbling out into the capacious glass placed to receive it. We had drawn first blood, and, with a 'dock-cellar' wave of the hand, the glass was temptingly held out to us. I was crafty enough to control my feelings enough not to take it. Jones had been there before, and I would watch him. I did so, and found that, at the docks, you never hold a glass by the stem, but take it by its foot between the thumb and fingers; it is well, too, if you wish to pass as a genuine connoisseur, to make much show of putting the wine before the lamp, and shutting one eye at it in a sort of confidential way. To skilfully spit out the first mouthful upon the sawdust is a good thing to do. The words 'dry', 'fruity', 'beeswing', 'crust', and 'bouquet', may be used with good effect, if you are sure you know what they mean. Robinson didn't know the other day, and so made himself silly before the cooper, by talking about the beeswing on the barrel. Of course my turn came to taste, and I did not hesitate to take it – my turn, and the wine too, for the matter of that. It amused me to see how admirably the cooper assumed a stolid belief that we were *bona fide* purchasers. If we had been George Sandeman himself, or Messrs Martinez and Co., in the flesh (which the Fates forfend!) he could not have been more serious with us. 'That, sir,' he would say, especially addressing me, after tasting, 'is No. 13; you will please remember, a fine East India Sherry.' 'Very good it is,' I would reply, smacking my lips approvingly, and looking at Jones, as much as to say, 'Be sure and get a pipe of that, partner, without fail!' I verily believe that innocent (if not hypocritical) cooper is expecting our order to come in to this day.

Shall I go on? I think I had better not. I shan't tell you how many barrels we stopped in front of before we left. In truth, I don't know nor does Robinson; and Jones won't say, so I don't think he knows either. I meant to make a long article out of the striking features of the vaults – the black cotton-wool fungus, like hearse feathers in a bad way, that clustered over and swung from the roof – the statistics of the wine stored there – the fabulous stories about certain treasured butts and prized pipes – the bibulous gossip of the

troglodytes who haunt the cellars – and so on; but, bless you, I find I know nothing about them. My advice to you is, don't mix your wines when you go to the docks, and, above all, don't drink Brandy on the top of them; that is, if you want to write instructive articles afterwards upon the subject.

from the *Figaro*

After recently spending a delightful and informative time in Burgundy with Trevor Hughes, visiting vineyards and tasting wines, I can well appreciate the author's difficulties, though in my own defence I must confirm that we were there on wholly legitimate grounds. The high point of the trip was undoubtedly a visit to the magnificent cellars of the Domaine de la Romanée-Conti. Before us were many barrels of the world's most expensive and precious wine, Romanée-Conti itself. For us their jewel was the 1993 La Tâche.

If sampling the wines presents no problem, I have a problem when visiting France, a country I know quite well and love. This is that having been an actor for more than twenty-five years I have developed a good ear for accents and have learnt, slowly and painfully at first, one of what I think are the golden rules of good acting, that is not 'to do it' but 'to be it'. So when in France I just think 'be a Frenchman'. As a result the few phrases I can speak such as 'How much is that piece of cheese?', 'Where is the Eiffel Tower?' and 'Do you enjoy cricket?' are delivered in faultless French. And here lies my dilemma – the performance is too good. My simple enquiry is invariably answered with a torrent of

friendly information about other cheeses and then more specific enquiries about I know not what. Having got away with a few grunts, snorts and 'Oui's' during the first phrase, the second brings hasty defeat. A look of mild irritation mixed with disappointment crosses the French person's face, the cheese is quickly brought and the Eiffel Tower is pointed out, dominating the nearby skyline.

My problem does not end there. More often than not I'm taken for a German! And on two occasions, both in deepest rural France, I have encountered French/German bilinguals. This really is awful. Having asked about the cheese and half-expecting a torrent of French I am answered with a torrent of German. Now I have a very rudimentary understanding of French, but apart from the numbers from one to ten, 'Ja', 'Nein', 'Danke schön', 'Schweinhund' and 'Donner und Blitzen' (the *Hotspur* comic has a lot to answer for) I have no German at all. In these circumstances I have to try to convey, midst a tidal wave of embarrassment, that I am not German, not even from Alsace. It quickly becomes all too apparent that the enquiry about the cheese is more or less the sum total of my French. I then emerge from the air-conditioned delicatessen, completely humbled and pouring with sweat, into the hot sunshine where almost immediately I am stung by a wasp on my left eyelid.

I trust that a glass of Château La Lagune, Ludon (Haut-Médoc), would soon help me overcome my embarrassment and possibly help me forget, if not forgive, the wasp.

Iram indeed is gone with all his Rose,
And Jamshyd's Sev'n-ring'd Cup where no one knows;
   But still a Ruby kindles in the Vine,
And many a Garden by the Water blows.

And David's lips are lockt; but in divine
High-piping Pehleví, with 'Wine! Wine! Wine!
   Red Wine!' – the Nightingale cries to the Rose
That sallow cheek of hers to' incarnadine.

A Book of Verses underneath the Bough,
A Jug of Wine, a Loaf of Bread – and Thou
   Beside me singing in the Wilderness –
Oh, Wilderness were Paradise enow!

Some for the Glories of This World; and some
Sigh for the Prophet's Paradise to come;
   Ah, take the Cash, and let the Credit go,
Nor heed the rumble of a distant Drum!

Look to the blowing Rose about us – 'Lo,
Laughing,' she says, 'into the world I blow,
   At once the silken tassel of my Purse
Tear, and its Treasure on the Garden throw.'

And those who husbanded the Golden grain,
And those who flung it to the winds like Rain,
   Alike to no such aureate Earth are turn'd
As, buried once, Men want dug up again.

Think, in this batter'd Caravanserai
Whose Portals are alternate Night and Day,
   How Sultán áfter Sultán with his Pomp
Abode his destined Hour, and went his way.

They say the Lion and the Lizard keep
The Courts where Jamshyd gloried and drank deep:
   And Bahrám, that great Hunter – the Wild Ass
Stamps o'er his Head, but cannot break his Sleep.

I sometimes think that never blows so red
The Rose as where some buried Cæsar bled;
   That every Hyacinth the Garden wears
Dropt in her Lap from some once lovely Head.

And this reviving Herb whose tender Green
Fledges the River-Lip on which we lean –
   Ah, lean upon it lightly! for who knows
From what once lovely Lip it springs unseen!

Ah, my Belovéd, fill the Cup that clears
TO-DAY of past Regrets and Future Fears:
   To-morrow! – Why, To-morrow I may be
Myself with Yesterday's Sev'n thousand Years.

For some we loved, the loveliest and the best
That from his Vintage rolling Time hath prest,
   Have drunk their Cup a Round or two before,
And one by one crept silently to rest.

And we, that now make merry in the Room
They left, and Summer dresses in new bloom,
   Ourselves must we beneath the Couch of Earth
Descend – ourselves to make a Couch – for whom?

Ah, make the most of what we yet may spend,
Before we too into the Dust descend;
   Dust into Dust, and under Dust to lie,
Sans Wine, sans Song, sans Singer, and – sans End! –

Yon rising Moon that looks for us again –
How oft hereafter will she wax and wane;
   How oft hereafter rising look for us
Through this same Garden – and for *one* in vain!

And when like her, oh Sákí, you shall pass
Among the Guests Star-scatter'd on the Grass,
    And in your joyous errand reach the spot
Where I made One – turn down an empty Glass!

Edward FitzGerald from *The Rubáiyát of Omar Khayyám,* 1859

With repeated references to the rose a pink champagne seems a must and André Clouet's Grand Cru Rosé from the village of Bouzy is a great favourite with all who have drunk it.

To go with FitzGerald, a long-hidden 'champagne memory' has emerged from the depths.

My father and mother had an actor friend called Kim Peacock. He was older than my parents and a good way to describe him would be to say that he was like a slightly camp Cary Grant. He was moderately successful as an actor but had to rely on his substantial private wealth. He lived in an exquisite flat overlooking the Thames at Kingston and once, on my way to school at the start of term, the dread journey was lightened by lunch cooked by Kim. He served a dish of sautéed chicken in champagne. This dish was made remarkable by the fact that you really could taste the champagne, not just a white wine but unmistakably champagne. That meal remains the most successful champagne cookery I've ever tasted.

One more quick story about Kim Peacock. In the very early sixties my parents and Kim went on holiday together. I can see them now setting off in Kim's white Mercedes convertible. The holiday was to consist of a leisurely drive through France and then a longer stay on the Italian Riviera. They had a whale of a time. The only thing that slightly shocked my father was Kim's bathing attire, described by him as a small blue lady's handkerchief secured by three thongs. You must remember that this was thirty-five years ago when things were very different, even on the Italian Riviera. The first time Kim appeared dressed like this, my father said, 'Kim, you really should cover up a little more.'

To which Kim replied, 'It's just a thought.'

POSTSCRIPT

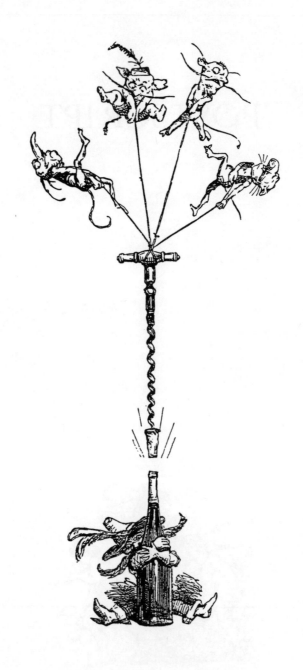

I've greatly enjoyed putting this book together. So maybe there'll be a sequel: *A Good Egg,* a collection of prose and poetry gathered over the years about eggs. It doesn't have quite the same fizz about it as this book and of course I don't want to yolk myself with an impossible task. (That, I promise you, is the only and certainly the last pun in this book.)

With reference to my golden rule about not drinking while I am working, my hand is already straying in the direction of the corkscrew. This recalls other drinks at the end of the working day, with which I'd like to leave you.

In 1972 I got the part of the 'juvenile' in William Douglas-Home's *Lloyd George Knew My Father.* The stars were Sir Ralph Richardson and Dame Peggy Ashcroft. When we'd settled into our run at the Savoy Theatre, Ralph invited me to have a drink with him after the show. This became a fairly regular occurrence, so in the year I was in the show with Ralph, I must have been to his dressing-room thirty or forty times.

The opening routine was always exactly the same. I'd knock at the door, which would be quickly opened by Hal, Ralph's dresser. Hal was barely five feet tall, very dapper, with a smiling but somehow scrunched-up face, a tan (more Max factor than Mother Nature) and a curious arrangement of red-coloured hair. He always reminded me of a hamster.

Ralph would be sitting at his dressing-table in a white towelling dressing-gown with the initials RR embroidered in blue on the left-hand side. As he saw me he'd say, 'Ah, it's the Boy.' (Ralph gave me the name very early on in rehearsals. I was only twenty-two!) The dialogue would then proceed as follows :

Ralph: Gin?

Me: Yes, please.

Ralph: Hal, gin for the Boy.

Hal would scurry over with two huge and beautiful crystal tumblers (Ralph lived in some opulence, there was a Turner hanging in his dressing-room) and a bottle of Gordon's. Ralph would pour a vast amount of gin into each glass.

Ralph: Tonic?

Me: Yes, please.

Ralph: Hal, tonic for the Boy.

Hal would bring the opened bottle of tonic. Ralph would take it and splash the tiniest amount of tonic into each glass. He'd hand me my glass and then without a word drain his. Hal quickly refilled it with the same proportions, four-fifths gin to one-fifth tonic, and as Ralph lifted it to his lips to take a small sip he would say, 'And now for pleasure.'

222

ACKNOWLEDGEMENTS

We gratefully acknowledge permission to reprint extracts of copyright material in this book from the following writers, publishers and literary representatives:

Wine Mine, November 1973, for an extract from *Sweet Vegetables, Soft Wines* by Elizabeth David, reprinted in *An Omelette and a Glass of Wine*, 1984, copyright Elizabeth David.

Dramatic Copyrights Limited, copyright 1991, for an extract by Christopher Fry from *Memorable Dinners*, published in aid of St John Ambulance, 1991.

Reed Consumer Books, for an extract from *Clochemerle* by Gabriel Chevallier, translated by Jocelyn Godefroi, published by Martin Secker & Warburg, 1985.

Sidgwick & Jackson, for extracts from *Wine With Food* by Cyril and Elizabeth Ray, 1975.

Headline Book Publishers Limited, for an extract from *Jancis Robinson's Food and Wine Adventures* by Jancis Robinson.

Weidenfeld & Nicolson, for an extract from *The Tuscan World* by Elizabeth Romer, 1984.

Michel Roux, for an extract from *Memorable Dinners,* published in aid of St John Ambulance, 1991.

Mrs J R Guillet, for extracts from *A Wine Primer* by André Simon, published by Michael Joseph Limited.

Wine Primer, Winter 1970, for an extract from a competition entry by A G Cairns Smith.